He Was Never a Cat

Knick's Story, My Story, Your Story

Booklocker.com, Inc.
2010

He Was Never a Cat

Knick's Story, My Story, Your Story

Patti Tingen

Paula,
Enjoy the stories!
Blessings,
Patti
12/3/11

Dedication

Father, Son and Holy Spirit—this book is Yours

Tony and Sharon—for your invaluable advice and expertise

Jeanie, Randy, Denise, Mom and Dad—for your love, support and encouragement

Doug—my best friend for over 25 years. I love you.

Knick—my "first best cat"—forever!

Table of Contents

Chapter 1

He was hungry...
Find your passion

Knick's Story:

He could devour a bowl of cat food with lightning-quick speed. His appetite was endless. His hunger knew no bounds. He begged without ceasing for his next meal. He would gobble up nearly anything he could find. His name was Knick—and he was unlike any cat I had ever met.

I had wanted a cat for many years, but due to living in rental properties throughout our marriage, it was never possible. Then in April of 1992 we bought our first home. We were there about a month when it suddenly dawned on me—"I can get a cat!"

So on that warm Sunday afternoon in May, I announced it to my husband Doug. "I'm going to get a cat."

"That's nice," he lazily replied, not wanting to be distracted from his television watching.

Grabbing my purse and car keys, I headed for the door.

"Hey—where are you going?!"

"I told you—to get a cat."

"Well yeah, but I didn't know you meant right now."

"Yes, right now. I've been playing long enough with strays on the sidewalk. I'm going to the Humane League."

Out of a litter of 9, he and his brother were the only two left. One a darker gray tabby, one lighter. I considered taking them both, but given the encouraging send-off from my spouse, I decided I best stick with just one. I chose the darker one. Off we went, he riding contentedly in his little cardboard box, me gleeful with joy at my first adult-owned pet. My little bundle of fur was 2 months old and could fit in the palm of my hand.

After a brief look around at his new environment, my little kitty strode toward the living room, ringed-tail held ramrod straight, as if he owned the place. He quickly found a seat on the back of the sofa and curled up for a nap.

Doug, still engrossed in his TV viewing, said, "Well, my New York Knickerbockers are playing the Chicago Bulls in the 7th game of the Eastern conference semi-finals—we can name him Knickerbocker—Knick for short. Maybe it will bring them luck." The Knicks lost 110-81.

Not knowing any better, I thought Knick could be one of those self-feeding cats. So I filled his little bowl with Kitten Chow™ and he ate from it. But when I began to prepare my own supper, suddenly I felt something crawling up the back of my pants, meowing its little head off. Upon being extricated from my leg, the little guy went up a few stairs near the stove, craning his neck high in the air to get a whiff of steam from the water I was boiling. "My gosh—what do you know about food?! You're barely off mother's milk!"

Doug made the unfortunate decision to take his dinner to the couch with him—within paw's reach of a certain little cat. One foot in the grilled cheese sandwich and a loud human cry later, my spouse's supper was in the trash.

"You didn't need to throw away the ENTIRE sandwich," I chastised.

"He stepped in it!"

"O relax, he's a kitten—you'll have this."

We quickly learned that Knick lived to eat. He'd wake up from a nap—he'd eat. He'd use the litter box—he'd eat. **I'd** go to the bathroom—he'd eat. I also learned that self-feeding (or more like continual-feeding in his case) was not going to work. So began our routine of regimented, portion-controlled meals.

As Knick grew in age, he also grew in stature. Thankfully he had a large frame with which to support his ever-growing bulk, but it was still quite evident that in spite of our regimented feeding schedule, our boy had a weight problem. This did not go unnoticed by his vet. Dr. Bill suggested that we start Knick on "light" cat food. He gained 4 pounds. Several years later, we moved to prescription diet food and our "Maxipuss" eventually slimmed down.

In his prime, Knick was quite the physical specimen. Standing at the dining room table, he could rest his large, round head on top of the surface with two massive gray paws framing his face. Tipping the scale at 18 pounds, his unending appetite never diminished. Knick knew the routine—he got fed 3 times per day. When I got up at 6 AM, when I returned from work at 5 PM and before bed at 10 PM. But that did nothing to deter the furry fellow from asking for his bowl to be filled at any other time as well. I know cats spend much of their time sleeping, but with Knick it almost seemed more like something to do to pass the time while waiting for his next meal. When he woke up from his nap, he was certain that it would be feeding time again.

When it wasn't, he voiced his displeasure quite vigorously—and continuously. Many evenings, once Doug and I were in our assigned places watching television, Knick would take his place at the end of our long living room. There he'd sit, plump body forming a perfect triangle, asking over and over again in full voice. *"Meow, meow, meow, meow, meow, meow, meow, meow, meow..."* He could literally keep that up for hours on end in spite of us never giving in. His persistence was admirable. I must admit, however, it was also highly annoying.

Mostly I just felt sorry for him. Those large gold eyes kept a constant vigil fixed on my every move. If I made even the slightest twitch that gave the appearance of leaving the recliner, he'd stand to his feet, ready to run towards his beloved rose-colored bowl. If I actually <u>did</u> get up, say to use the bathroom, or perhaps to get myself a snack, his reaction increased ten-fold. *"MEOW, MEOW, MEOW..."*

"No Knickie, it's not time yet."

After dutifully accompanying me to whatever task I might have completed, he'd once again assume the position—both in posture and voice.

Knick's passion for food was unstoppable, no matter the circumstances. One time, after returning home from surgery to have a cyst removed from his leg, he immediately went to his dishes in spite of his post-anesthetic stupor. Of course we gave him a small snack—comfort food after his medical ordeal. In he went with his usual vigor—and more noise than I would have ever thought a cat could make, especially while eating. *"MAU, MAU, MAU, MAU, MAU, MAU, MAU..."* It was a combination of "Meow" and "Ow" rolled into one—at an unbelievable volume!

After finishing off the food, he dove into his water dish—almost literally. Still groggy, his head fell forward into his bowl and we seriously thought he might drown. But he just needed to wash down his meal. After that, he began to take a few wobbly steps into the kitchen. Getting no further than the stove, he paused to look back. Eyes still glazed over, he gave his wanderings a second thought. *"I better not stray too far from here."* Making it back successfully to his feeding area, our sweet Knickie curled up for the night, his precious dishes not more than 2 feet in front of him.

Our feline was checked medically for any sort of chemical imbalance or thyroid issue, but nothing was found. He was simply hungry—all the time. Poor Knick was so desperate he would eat anything he could find, including fuzzies and even his own shed toenails!

Knick also had quite a penchant for plastic grocery bags. We never figured out if it was the lingering smell of food, or what it was, but he absolutely loved crawling inside the bags—and LICKING the insides of them! Sitting with the bag entirely covering his body, he'd slurp away, round cat face pressed tight against the side of the bag, pink tongue licking madly at the plastic. (Knick enjoyed other activities with plastic bags as well, but that's for another chapter.)

In addition to non-edibles, Knick also took advantage of every available opportunity to obtain any sort of "people" food, even though we were very diligent in never purposefully sharing our bounty with him. Doug had an unfortunate habit of leaving the table in the middle of his meal, and "you know who" never missed the chance at an unmanned plate.

One night I had made little mini-pizzas out of pita bread. Sure enough, Doug left his place for some reason, and upon return, there he was. Seated in the chair, his large, gray head resting just above the table—with a small rectangle of cheese pizza dangling from his lips. Although he never really had a full slice, pizza was definitely on our boy's top ten food list.

One evening I made the mistake of placing an empty carry-out box next to our sturdy wooden trash can, the box wedged tightly between the wall and the can. A loud crash later, I arrived to find one large tabby standing in the middle of the folded cardboard, licking grease as quickly as his rough-edged tongue could carry him.

On another occasion, the boy swiped a piece of pork chop fat. I found him under the table, lips smacking, slobber flowing, as he tried in vain to get it chewed and swallowed before it was too late.

Thankfully I was able to reach into his mouth and extract the piece before it had the chance to get lodged in his little kitty throat.

One of our favorite Knick stories involves his once in a lifetime opportunity to gorge himself with absolutely no end in sight. We kept some food in a plastic container in the kitchen closet to use day to day, but we always kept the bag of cat food on the basement steps, behind closed doors and out of kitty's reach.

For some reason on that fateful day, I brought a brand new 20-lb. bag home and left it in the mud room, right inside the back door. Later, I went away for the evening, leaving Knick in my capable husband's hands. Looking back on it, Doug says that he hadn't seen much of him that evening, and assumed that he was sitting on his table in the back room, awaiting my return. To him, the only sign of Knick's presence that night was the large pile of vomit that he left in the kitchen at one point.

Needless to say, I was taken aback when I walked through the back door a few hours later. There he was—in full glory—sitting in front of his bag of Heaven—large round hole chewed and clawed through at PERFECT feeding height—eating to his heart's content!! Already gapping and swallowing as fast as possible, knowing that it was only a matter of time before the gig was up, Knick increased his pace, if it was even possible, the second he saw me coming.

Of course, my first instinct was to yell. "Doug!!!" "Do you know what he's doing?"

"What? No—I know he threw up."

"How could you not know he was doing this?!"

Meanwhile, Knick was continuing his inhaling.

Quickly I grabbed some tape and worked on sealing off his opening, all the while needing to fight against his furry face even more furiously trying to get some last morsels before his feeding frenzy was over.

That night convinced me that Knick truly had no satiation point. I honestly believe he would have ate and puked and ate and puked until he finished off the complete bag if I hadn't returned home. It goes without saying that that was the last time I forgot to put the new bag of cat food away.

My Story:

So what can we learn from Knick's insatiable appetite? Well certainly he shows us what passion looks like. His desire and drive for food was unstoppable.

I had never been a particularly passionate person. Doug would often ask me, "What are your hopes, your dreams? What's your passion?"

And my response was usually, "I don't know. I just kind of go with the flow. Yeah, I have some ideas of things I'd like, but overall I'm pretty content just seeing what each day brings."

He would just sigh and shake his head.

Unfortunately, that blandness began to carry over into my spiritual life as well. I'd been a Christian since I was a child, and my faith really grew during my college years. But after settling into marriage and a job, my relationship with Christ began to get stale.

If you had asked me, I certainly would have said that I loved God—and I did! But I thought the real spiritual way of living was kind of reserved for pastors or other church staff. I thought it was a little too much for regular people like me. Besides, I thought, they do that church stuff all week long—that's their job—so of course they're going to be closer to God than the rest of us.

That seemed like a good theory to me—until I saw Doug really starting to grow spiritually. Then I was kind of getting stuck. I found myself in this in-between place where I was feeling more and more uncomfortable. I thought, "I'm okay with how I'm living, aren't I? Can I really get that excited about God? I'm not sure I want to go there; that just seems a bit too fanatical for me."

But then God stepped in and gave me revelation and He changed my heart. He helped me to see that along with my husband, some of my friends were going on in a deeper relationship with Him and that our church was moving ahead as well. I thought, "Gosh, I do not want to be stuck in this wishy-washy, kind of halfway-there, lukewarm Christianity." I knew that I could no longer sit on the fence.

So on July 6, 1997, I decided to give myself fully to Christ and seek Him with a hunger like never before. It was amazing! I understood in a way that I never had before that I was a sinner and that I really was not good enough on my own. For the first time in my life, I finally understood why I needed Christ. The road after that decision has not been easy by any means, but I've never looked back. God honored my choice and put me on a path of which I never would have dreamed.

Finally—I had some understanding of passion.

Your Story:

What is your passion? Do you even have one? Or are you like I was, living a blah, kind of day to day existence? If you do know your passion, how vigorously are you pursuing it? With the same fervor and drive that Knick desired food? What if you did? How would that decision impact your life as well as those around you?

One of the Beatitudes says, "Blessed are those who hunger and thirst for righteousness, for they will be filled." (Matthew 5:6, NIV)

What if you pursued God with the kind of passion that Knick had for food? What might our world look like if all of us had even a small portion of that kind of hunger for righteousness? The best part is that Scripture promises that if we do this, we will be filled, unlike poor Knick's ever-present hunger. But his laser-focused drive and determination can give us a picture of what that type of "hunger" might look like.

God is looking for believers with passion. He wants followers who will love boldly, serve energetically and follow Him fully. Our Lord despises half-heartedness.

Revelation 3:15-16 (NIV) states, "I know your deeds, that you are neither cold nor hot. I wish you were either one or the other! So, because you are lukewarm—neither hot nor cold—I am about to spit you out of my mouth."

Those are strong words and we would do well to take them seriously. I greatly encourage you to take an honest look at your relationship with God. Are you leaving a bad taste in His mouth because of your tepid lifestyle?

You have no idea what far-reaching plans God may have in store for you. But in order to find out, you need to begin or continue the process of discerning and following your passion. If you're content to continue in your bland existence, not understanding your purpose in life, you'll never fully experience all that God has for you.

Our greatest desire should be the pursuit of our relationship with Christ. Then from that passion will flow our gifts, talents and opportunities to serve and bless others in the way that He is calling us. But in all of this, there needs to be a balance. As we discovered with Knick, his appetite for food was so strong that it was actually unhealthy for him. He became overweight and also proved that he would literally eat himself sick if given the opportunity.

As vital as it is to pursue your dreams and desires, there also needs to be some perspective. When the pursuit of something becomes all encompassing and the drive towards that goal, whatever it might be, becomes your only focus, it's time to take a step back and reevaluate.

Are you pursuing your career with so much passion that you're neglecting your relationship with your spouse and children? Is your desire for money greater than your longing for spiritual riches? In your fervor for giving and serving others, even through service in the church, are you inattentive to your health or your own family's needs?

No matter what our passion or pursuit—if it's out of balance—we're not helping anyone. We need to constantly be checking our motives, desires and actions to insure that they remain pure and focused on the ultimate goal.

Jesus said that the greatest commandment is to "Love the Lord your God with all your heart and with all your soul and with all your mind." Then to "Love your neighbor as yourself." (Matthew 22:37-38, NIV)

Let those commandments be your guide.

If you've never entered into a relationship with Jesus, all you need to do is ask. One sincere "Meow" will do it. Acknowledging your sins and Christ's death and resurrection in paying the penalty for them is all that's needed. And you can begin the adventure of a lifetime!

If you're already a believer, but have lost your passion somewhere along the way, it's never too late to rekindle the flame. I can certainly testify to that. Let your lips water and your stomach yearn for food that will really satisfy. Hunger once again for your first Love with all the determination that your Knick-like soul can muster.

Chapter 2

He was talkative...
Choose your words carefully

Knick's Story:

Like most things Knick, they were carried out with gusto and pushed to the maximum limit. He was passionate about nearly everything. "Speaking" was no exception.

As much as our kitty loved eating, the boy also loved to talk. He had the full repertoire of cat sounds and then some. Knick was constantly yapping his lips—he talked to Doug and me all the time and especially in his later years, we'd hear him talking to himself. It never happened, but had he uttered a full sentence in perfect English, I never would have batted an eye.

As previously noted, most of Knick's chattiness involved his requests for food. I'm not sure why I ever bothered setting a clock, because I already had a ready-made striped tabby alarm who "went off" without fail every day at 6 AM if not earlier. Most times he'd plant himself on the bedside stand to do his early morning crowing. But occasionally he'd sit on the stairs that opened up into our bedroom. *"Meow, meow, meow, meow..."*

A strategy that sent him scurrying the first few times I used it was to throw a slipper at him. Of course Knick was onto my tricks in no time; he'd duck below the first step and the slipper would go flying over his head and down the stairs. After two ducks, I was out of slippers but he had an unlimited supply of *"Meows"* left. How he never went hoarse is still a mystery to me.

The "fall back" time change was always the worst. Of course when his stomach went off at 6:00 "Knick-time", it was only 5:00 "Patti-time." He comprehended so much of what I told him, but he was never able to get the time change thing down. Usually I couldn't stand listening to him for a whole hour, so I'd give in around 5:30 and slowly work him back to his regular schedule over a few days time. Obviously he LOVED that magical day in spring when seemingly out of nowhere, it was already time to eat!

As much as we sometimes tired of Knickie's continual chatter, there were times when it came in handy for him. One day our world seemed strangely quiet. Wandering into the living room, I thought I heard something. *"Mewww, mewww, mewww..."* It sounded like Knick yet strangely muffled. Then I realized that the cries were coming from the recliner. Quickly I opened up the footrest and as if by magic, a large furball suddenly appeared out of the piece of furniture.

He'd yap one word sounds to Doug, but Knick and me, we could carry on complete conversations.

"Maw!"

"What Knickie?"

"MAW!! MAW!!"

"What do you want?"

Often he'd go to his dish, but sometimes he'd stroll to the back door. *"MAWR!!!"*

Depending on my mood, his mood, the weather and any number of other factors, I might give in. The rules for going outside were that Knick was not allowed to go anywhere beyond the fenced-in deck. Most of the time he was content with that and was happy to just lay down and get some sun on his belly. Unfortunately, I was usually ready to come back inside long before he was.

"Okay Knick, we need to go in."

"MAWR!"

"Yes, we've been out long enough, come on…" With that, I'd open the door and start to go inside. Sometimes we'd argue a bit and on other occasions, he was more responsive. But eventually he would always follow—making his disapproval known with each step as he waddled down the stairs of the deck and into the house. In rapid fire, short, staccato-like bursts, Knick would express his displeasure. *"Mawrp. Mawrp-mawrp-mawrp. MAWRP-MAWRP-MAWRP-MAWRP-MAWRP-MAWRP-MAWRP!!!"*

Doug and I used to call it "cat cursing." And our boy could be pretty foul-mouthed. The type of sounds he could make and the speed at which he'd spit them out was just hilarious!

It always made me laugh that Knick was so compliant for as much as he complained about things. Whether it was going back inside, needing some sort of home medical care or even going to the vet, I can't remember one time when my fuzzy friend didn't come to me when I called. No matter where he was in the house, even if taking a long winter's nap, if I called for him to come, he'd be there. Sometimes with quite a look of weariness, but still a sense of *"I'm here – what do you need?"*

It always broke my heart when it was "vet-time" and I'd need to pick him up and stuff him in his carrier, while a loud cry of *"NOOOOOOOOO!!!!!"* emanated from his lips. Then he'd hyperventilate for the entire 2-mile drive to and from the doctor's. Poor thing—I always wondered if I should have given him a little paper bag to try and breathe into.

Even as a kitten, Knick made his presence known at Dr. Bill's. At the tender age of 6 months, there was no doubt that our fella was all boy. It was time for "the removal." The vet tech said she would call when he could be picked up. I was both surprised and amused when the phone rang earlier than expected and a very exasperated voice said, "He's ready. Come get him!" She left out the "PLEASE" but I could hear it in her voice. *"Meow, meow, meow, meow..."* was driving them all crazy.

An activity that I thought was quite clever was having Knick help to make our answering machine messages. One of them involved us all saying our names. I would start—"Hi, this is Patti, 'Doug' (spoken by Doug) and *"MAAUUUWWW!"* (spoken by you know who). Strangely enough, it was always one of the few times when Knick didn't feel like being verbal. It probably took us at least 10 "takes" to do that particular message. One of us would mess up or there would be too long of a pause between our names or "someone" wouldn't speak when it was his turn. But again, my buddy was fully cooperative, letting me hold him, and eventually getting the idea that when I squeezed his belly and jostled him a bit, that meant he was supposed to say *"Knick."* It was a great message.

But my favorite one went like this—"Hi! This is Patti and Doug; we're not home right now, so at the sound of Knick, please leave a message. *"MEOWWWW!!"* He hit his cue perfectly on that one! Even one of the telemarketers enjoyed it. I don't know why the guy was actually calling, but what was recorded on our machine was, "At the sound of Knick—that's great!!" followed by much laughter.

Knick maintained his chatty nature throughout his lifetime, but as we all do as we age, sometimes he would get confused. Often I would be sitting at the dining room table when Knickie came sauntering past. Of course to be polite, I would say "Hi Knick!" as he was going by. Which of course caused him to offer a return hello. Unfortunately, in his older age, it also caused him to stop dead in his tracks and forget what it was he was doing or where he was going. After a few seconds of desperate looking around and with a confused and embarrassed look, he'd make an about-face and go back towards the living room, mumbling to himself as he went. *"Mehh mehh mehh*

mehh mehh..." Which I interpreted as, "*Shoot! Where was I going? Oh forget it. I'll just go back to where I came from.*"

My Story:

What insight can we gain from Knick's chatty nature? Well the Bible has much to say about our mouths and our tongues. In fact the entire 3rd chapter of James is about our tongues—and how praise and cursing can come out of the same mouth.

Knick certainly proved that. He could "cat curse" with the best of them. But his sweet meows and loving purrs came from the same place. I'm no different. Out of my mouth can flow beautiful words of comfort, encouragement and praise—or out can come gossip and criticism.

What we say can either build others up or tear them down. It doesn't take much. One word can bring healing and hope. Or with one word, we can hurt, devastate and destroy. The Book of James also says, "the tongue is a small thing, but what enormous damage it can do."

Our words—whether one or many, positive or negative—are powerful.

As you'll read in the next chapter, I've been deeply hurt by the words of others. Yet I continue to struggle with my own tongue. I absolutely agree with this Scripture—"no man can tame the tongue. It is a restless evil, full of deadly poison." (James 3:8, NIV)

As much as errant talk and hateful slander have wounded me, I still find myself speaking negative words about others or willingly listening to the latest gossip. Although much of the talk may never even reach the ears of the person being spoken about, those words wound and hurt nonetheless. Just the fact that they are spoken at all is enough to cause damage.

I would do well to follow the parameters outlined in Ephesians 4:29 (NIV). "Do not let any unwholesome talk come out of your mouths, but only what is helpful for building others up according to their needs, that it may benefit those who listen."

Doug has said many times that his mother always told him, "If you don't have anything good to say, don't say anything at all." Edna was a very wise woman and she left behind a beautiful legacy and many admonitions worth following.

There are words that are better left unspoken and there are words that need to be spoken but never are. The following is an incredibly sad example of the latter.

"When a corporate accountant committed suicide, an effort was made to find out why. The company's books were examined, but no shortage was found. Nothing could be uncovered that gave any clue as to why he took his life—that is, until a note was discovered. It simply said: "In 30 years I have never had one word of encouragement. I'm fed up!" [1]

One word would have saved that man's life! Don't think your words mean much? Think again. The impact we can have on each other's lives with just a few words is incredible. It's priceless. And we need to use every opportunity we have to speak words that will bring health and healing and life to those around us.

Also, don't ever be surprised at what God might want you to do with your mouth. Back in September of 1999, I was taking a Sunday afternoon nap and right before I woke up, I dreamt that I had fishing line and hooks all stuck in my tongue. Upon waking, my first thought was, "I'm going to be a fisher of men—and I'll catch them with my tongue."

That seemed pretty exciting. I pictured God giving me more opportunities to talk to people about Him—like neighbors or co-workers—one-on-one conversations. Well imagine my surprise when one year later, I was preaching an entire 30-minute sermon in two Sunday morning church services! I didn't know He meant my tongue would be in public!

I don't do public speaking. At least I never did—or thought I would—but Someone had other ideas. It started out when God gave

---

[1] Our Daily Bread, July 7, 2003

me some thoughts on giving, so I presented them before we took up the offering one Sunday morning at church. Then about a year later I gave the greeting at the beginning of a service. After giving another offering, Doug said, "You know you have a teaching gift."

I said, "No I don't."

He said, "Yes you do."

I said, "No, I have an—every now and then when God gives me something to say I'll do the offering—gift."

He said, "There is no such gift."

And I said, "Yes there is, and I have it."

Yet I had to admit, there were words that God wanted spoken through me—and I was the only one who could say them. So I decided to cooperate—and it's been the most amazing experience of my life. I've taught at church an average of once a year, sometimes twice. God has allowed me to speak from my life experiences and as a result, those words have been able to bring comfort, encouragement and hope to many, many people.

I am in total awe that He would use me to bring those words to so many folks. Unlike my Knick, I'm pretty quiet by nature. But when my Owner gently squeezes my belly just right, sounds come out. And He makes sure the message is perfect every time.

Your Story:

Now it's your turn. Like Knick, are you chatty by nature or do you tend to be more on the quiet side like me? Our words may be many or they may be few, but if it's the same old "Meow" passing through our lips over and over again, after awhile, others will tire of hearing them.

Hopefully you'll never have a slipper thrown at your head, but have you ever had your spouse or one of your children shut you out because they've had enough of your nagging or complaining? Maybe you cringe when you see a certain neighbor or co-worker coming your way, because you know they're going to talk your ear off and you're simply tired of their ramblings. Perhaps you're the irritating neighbor or co-worker.

God wants us to use our mouths to bless others and not to hurt them. We're all familiar with the old "sticks and stones" rhyme and we all know that "words will never hurt me" is an absolute lie. We've all been harmed by the words of others. Words cut to the core of our beings and are never forgotten.

I imagine most of us can remember words spoken to us or about us by parents, teachers, or peers like it was yesterday—even if it was 30 years ago. Childhood hurts can still sting our eyes like they did in grade school. To the contrary, words of encouragement, support and hope can fill our hearts with gratitude and thanks as we remember the precise quotes spoken to us in love.

How are you doing in this area? Are your words helpful for encouraging others and building them up? Or do they more often bring others down? Let angry thoughts and words fall by the wayside. Use your mouth to bring life and hope and healing to others. Let expressions of kindness, comfort and blessing be on your lips at all times. Speak a word of encouragement to those around you. Who knows—you just may end up saving a life?

Although there is a time to speak, we also need to recognize that there is a time to remain quiet. Sometimes, the best words of all are those that are never spoken. A sincere, listening ear can go a long way towards blessing someone who is hurting. You might not have the right words to say, but often, not saying anything is exactly what is needed.

For instance, after the unexpected death of a loved one, often what the grieving individual needs is just a hand to hold and a shoulder to cry on. Spouting Scripture and offering all kinds of platitudes is usually not helpful, even if said with every good intention. Offering a listening ear, uncomfortable as it might seem, is usually what is most appreciated.

Whether speaking or listening, what's in our hearts is most important. For that is where our words originate. Matthew 12:34 says, "For out of the overflow of the heart, the mouth speaks." (NIV)

Do you have a loving heart that spills over with kind and gentle words? Is your heart open to allowing God to use not only your tongue, but also your entire life in whatever way He determines is best?

We each have a story—and we are the only ones who can tell that story. Because it's unique to us. There might be similarities, but each one of us has a specific combination of background, personality and experiences that makes us uniquely us.

What individualized gifts and talents has He given you to carry out His work? What might God be asking of you that only you could accomplish? We so easily become jealous of someone else's looks or talents or situations. We think, "If only I could be that person—all would be well." But it wouldn't. Because that person has his or her own set of problems.

Relax and let God help you become all that He has created you to be. Let Him mold you, use you and speak through you however He chooses. All you need to do is cooperate with the One who created you. Focus your thoughts and energies on loving Him and being the unique person that He's created you to be. He'll do the rest—in His time and in His way.

One of the best ways to hear what God might be asking of you is to spend some time with Him in stillness. For it's in the silence that we can best hear from Him. "Be still and know that I am God." (Psalm 46:10, NIV) It's awfully hard to hear that still, small voice when we're making too much of our own noise.

So learn how to listen. It doesn't necessarily mean you need to find a completely quiet place to just sit in silence although that certainly is helpful. But it might just mean turning off the thoughts going through your mind so you can be open to hear what words the Holy Spirit might be gently whispering in your ear.

But also know that God does love when we talk to Him. He longs for us to have a relationship with Him and to tell Him every detail of our lives. He wants nothing more than for us to pour out our dreams, longings, hurts and disappointments to Him. 1 Thessalonians 5:17 (NAS) says "Pray without ceasing." "*Meow, meow, meow, meow…*"

God longs for us to tell Him the desires of our hearts, to ask and keep asking, to seek and keep seeking. He never grows tired or weary of our requests—even if we constantly beg over and over again. But we also need to keep in mind that He knows what's best for us. He knows exactly when and how much to "feed" us. Even though our internal clocks may say it's time, only He determines when to fill our bowls. If we can learn to rest in that, which is a lesson Knickerbocker never learned, maybe we can move from the same old "Meow" over and over again to a deeper, more meaningful relationship—but without losing that constant, ongoing dialogue with our Savior.

Chapter 3

He was intimidating...
Understand your foes

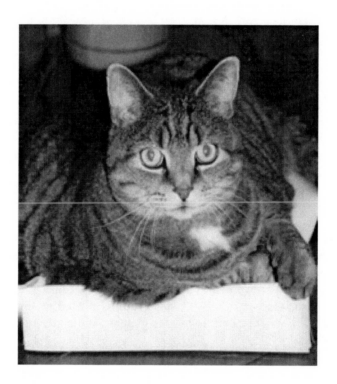

Knick's Story:

Obviously Knick's size alone was enough to make people wary of him; it didn't help that he also had an attitude at times, coupled with an ability to stare down even the best of them.

Knick absolutely adored me. Doug he tolerated until later in their relationship when they had a breakthrough and finally became the best of buddies. As far as most anyone else—they just seemed to be an annoyance to him.

Knick made it his practice to thoroughly inspect anyone who ventured into his domain. This was done mostly by staring at them—continuously—for as long as their visit lasted. Some people didn't really care—others were somewhat unnerved by it.

Doug's nephew fell into the latter category. Jason came for a visit one weekend. Neither he nor Knick had ever laid eyes on one another. Jason was immediately impressed by our big boy's size—"Holy cow! He takes up an entire sofa cushion!" Which he did. But that was nothing compared to what lay ahead.

Poor Jason barely got a wink of sleep that night. He slept (figuratively speaking) on the couch and just a stone's throw away sat the cat king—watching over this unknown from dusk to dawn. The next morning we innocently came downstairs, wondering if the young man had a comfortable rest. "I couldn't get any sleep—he was staring at me all night long!" When we drove Jason back to his trade school that afternoon, the poor kid snoozed for the entire 2-hour trip.

Just for fun, I would periodically enter into staring contests with Knick. I never won; I'd blink first every time. I don't know how his eyeballs didn't dry out, but he could keep those big round eyes wide open for a seemingly endless length of time. It was especially scary at night—even for me. I'd roll over in bed, and there sat that huge furry triangle on the nightstand, pupils dilated to the size of nickels, like a massive owl, gold eyes glowing in the greenish light of the clock radio.

"Meow, meow, meow, meow…"

"No! It's not 6:00 yet!!"

Another frightening bedtime event was when Knick would come upstairs in the middle of the night. On numerous occasions, the sound of footsteps and the creak of the wooden stairs would startle either Doug or me awake. *Boof, boof, creak, boof, creak, boof…*

"Oh my gosh!!! Is it a burglar? Is it Doug? No he's here beside me. But I'm definitely hearing footsteps." Frozen with fear, my fuzzy mind racing, heart pounding...

BOOF!! He'd land on the bed with a thud.

"Oh alright—it's just Knick. It's okay... it's okay..."

One of Knick's pleasures was lying in the windowsill of the bedroom on a summer day, letting the breeze blow through his belly fur. On one particular day, I heard some talking and looked out. The neighbor girl was sitting in her open window with her legs dangling out, feet propped on the roof, chatting away on the phone. "Oh—you should see—there's a cat in the window of the house next door. Oh he's so cute! 'Hi kitty!' Hey—he's staring at me! Stop staring at me cat. Stop it! Stop it!!"

I peeked out just in time to see her legs retreat back inside the house. "Scared away another one. You go Knick!"

Along with his staring, Knick was also pretty good at the hiss. At his vet appointments, Dr. Bill never tried to complete a full inspection of his mouth. He'd just invade Knick's personal space close enough to get a good *"Heeehhhh"* out of him, take a quick glance at his bared fangs and say, "Teeth look good to me."

For the most part, Knick wouldn't hiss at someone unless he really felt cornered. My brother was the rare exception. Knick could be across the room when he walked in and Randy, in the sweetest, gentlest voice imaginable, would softly offer, "Hi Knickie."

"Heeehhhh."

I always thought it was that he smelled like children. Doug and I never had kids so they weren't a species with which our kitty was very familiar. But occasionally my niece and nephew would visit and it was enough to send the furball scurrying. Even Knick wasn't brave enough to stand up to them. Of course, they'd play with his toys and spin around in his little fleece bed. Poor kids—we didn't have any actual children's toys—what else were they supposed to do? When they'd finally clear out, Knick would cautiously creep about, inspect his property and get it sufficiently re-marked with his own scent. So even when Randy came alone, he would pay the penalty.

Occasionally we'd go away on vacation and someone would need to come in once a day to care for the boy. We enlisted several different brave souls to help with the task. But Knick's reaction was pretty much the same no matter who it was. *"Just put the food in the dish, get out of the way and no one gets hurt!"*

We did have one friend who Knick actually took a liking to. Karin and only one other person were the only two folks other than Doug and I, that he ever let pet him. But after a few days, even Karin would get the cold shoulder. She said she could see it in his eyes. *"Oh—it's you again. I don't want YOU! I want my mom!!"*

Yes, our Knick could present himself as quite a fearsome predator. Although I hate to admit this, in some circumstances and with some people, I think he was just plain nasty. But overall, I believe that more than anything, he was mostly just scared. Underneath all that great big bravado lay a cowardly lion who really just needed some courage.

My Story:

So what should we pick up from this Knick characteristic? To be intimidating to most everyone we come in contact with? Probably not, as fun as that might sound. But I think it can give us some insight into what lies beneath those fear-inducing personality types. You know who I'm talking about. The neighborhood bully, the relative that makes the whole family cringe, the supervisor who seems to hate everyone, that disagreeable co-worker... We've all run into them at one time or another. And it's a nightmare to put up with their glares, nasty looks, hissing comments and their overall intimidating presence.

Many years ago, I encountered some of these intimidating types in my workplace. Although I had the full support of my superiors, it did nothing to stem the tide of hurtful scowls, critical remarks and backstabbing strategies that were continually thrown my way. It appeared that every word I spoke and everything I did was dissected, analyzed and scrutinized. Nothing I did ever seemed good enough for these folks.

Another of the Beatitudes says, "Blessed are those who are persecuted because of righteousness, for theirs is the kingdom of heaven." (Matthew 5:10, NIV)

Although the hurts I suffered through this situation didn't come as a direct result of me speaking about my faith, I believe in a way they did come about because of who I was in Christ. From day one, I attempted to treat everyone equally, and to the best of my ability, I acted with honesty and integrity in every situation. Unfortunately, that didn't always seem to be appreciated.

Although the intensity of cruelty ebbed and flowed, the underlying current of intimidation continued on—day after day, week after week, and year after year. You might be wondering why I didn't just quit. Doug wondered that too. Many, many times. But every time my answer was the same. "Because I haven't done anything wrong! And I'm not going to let them push me out. I can last longer than them." And I did. I outlasted them all.

Then—I was given the opportunity to take a different job. I liked to think of it as my reward. My blessing for all the horrible years that I endured. But my blessing didn't just start when I got that new position. My blessing was there all along.

God's blessing was with me every day. He blessed me with a supervisor who had the courage to sacrifice one of her own friendships in order to support me whom she had only known for a brief time. God gave me a husband who patiently listened to my seemingly endless woes day after day. My Lord blessed me with the emotional strength to get up and drive to work Monday through Friday. His invisible presence was by my side every moment of every single day. He caught every tear that I ever cried during those many difficult years.

Who better would know the sting of persecution? The One who was vilified, spit upon, lied about, beaten, and eventually crucified. Jesus—who truly had done nothing to deserve the persecution He endured. And it was all of us who did that to Him. We persecuted Him—with our sins and all of our wrongdoings. But His response was love, nothing but love. He loved us enough to die for us.

Dealing with that level of intimidation day after day was certainly not easy. But along with the support I already described, one of the things that helped me was to recognize what lay beneath my foes' exterior. Like Knick, I believe the main component was fear. Feeling insecure and backed into a corner—they lashed out—teeth bared and claws exposed.

Unfortunately, as a result of what I suffered, I began to show some intimidation of my own at times. And my Knick-like self could be pretty fearsome as well. From a human perspective, my feelings and desire for retribution were absolutely justified. I had every right to enjoy every piece of revenge that came my way. But it's not God's way—and it's not the way of blessing—for myself or for others. So again and again, I'd repent and start over. And little by little, things got better. But those roots run deep and there were still some in me.

Then finally, after 10 years or more of working through the pain and hurt, and making the choice to forgive, over and over and over again—God finally and fully completed His healing in me. I also learned that I didn't need to prove myself or find my worth in someone else's approval. I'm good enough for God—and that's all that really matters.

Your Story:

How about you? Is there an intimidating "feline" in your life right now? Do you have hurts and pain from years ago that you haven't yet worked through? Are there people you need to forgive even if it's for the umpteenth time? Do you need to know God's strength in a greater way to get you through those troublesome times?

Whatever your situation—know that there is hope. In your difficult circumstances, know that Jesus is by your side. Know that He's blessing you—both now and for the future. In my own struggles, sometimes I recognized His blessings and sometimes I didn't, but He was there for the entire journey nonetheless.

It's always easier to look at things in hindsight, but don't neglect the opportunities to explore the blessings in the midst of your troubles as well. Use your spiritual eyes to see past the hurt and pain long enough to recognize what else might be going on that you can't see with your physical eyes. Our Lord is always present—and He knows our sorrows.

Also know that He feels your hurts more deeply than anyone else ever could. Know that His healing is there for you as well—no matter how long that healing may take. Sometimes it takes a very long time for those wounds to heal and to finally let go of the bitter roots of harshly spoken words, as we looked at in the last chapter. It took me over 10 years. It might take you longer. But keep working at it.

Jesus taught that we should forgive others 70 x 7. He didn't mean that when we got to 490, we could stop. He's implying that we need to forgive over and over and over again, for as long as it takes.

Recognize that forgiveness and healing is a process. The journey begins with the first step of choosing to take the difficult road of forgiveness. Don't become discouraged or feel guilty when those negative feelings rise to the surface again and again, even though you thought you had dealt with them. It's like the old example of peeling an onion. Just keep peeling and peeling. Though your eyes may burn and tears may stain your cheeks, continue to peel through the layers bit by bit, as much as you can take at one time. You'll know when you're ready for the next layer to come off. When it's time, continue on in the process. And through it all, recognize that you have a God who loves you and is leading you step by step.

If you're still in the midst of the tribulation, know that you are not alone—Jesus is by your side every single day. Trust Him, seek Him, love Him.

Continuing in Matthew 5, verses 10-11 say, "Blessed are you when people insult you, persecute you and falsely say all kinds of evil against you because of Me. Rejoice and be glad, because great is your reward in heaven, for in the same way they persecuted the prophets who were before you." (NIV)

So continue to persevere, because <u>great</u> will be your reward. Also recognize that your "bully" is probably dealing with fear and hurts in his or her own life. Although it's not easy, try to be understanding and give as much grace as possible. Gaining some perspective on how they may be feeling could be very beneficial in helping you deal with your own pain.

On the flip side, maybe you recognized yourself as the intimidator. Have you perfected the long, hard stare that immediately causes others to be afraid? Are you actually acting out of fear in yourself when you lash out at others? Would you like to be in a place where you have more than only two or three people that you feel completely comfortable with?

Take your hurts and pain to Christ as well. Confide in a friend, pastor or counselor who can help you to gain insight into why you treat others in that way. Pray through any past issues so you can learn to see yourself and others the way God sees you. With love. Trust that there is a better, more blessed way to live.

We will all deal with some scary "Knick's" at one point or another in our lives. If we can look past the intimidating outer shell long enough to see the scared inner kitty, perhaps we can find some compassion and love—and that will go a long way no matter what the circumstance.

Chapter 4

He was wimpy...
Face your fears courageously

Knick's Story:

As intimidating and fearsome as Knick could appear, not only was he a cowardly lion—he was also remarkably wimpy. For one thing, he was constantly cold. You would think given his size and the amount of fat covering his body, that the boy would have generated plenty of heat to keep himself toasty warm. However, this was not the case. All winter long, Knick would plant himself on the braided rug underneath the dining room table, right in front of the best heating vent in the house. There he'd wait patiently for the roar of the old furnace to kick on, knowing that shortly thereafter, the beautiful warmth of heated air would be his to enjoy. He'd lie by that vent for hours on end, just waiting for the next cycle to come around.

We lived in a very old house. It was a story and a half, with no attic and no insulation—in the walls or the roof. And for at least our first year in the home, we had no heat upstairs. I spent plenty of time with Knick in front of that vent as well! In the summer, Knick was in his glory, as we also had no air conditioning for several years. I desperately wish we could have figured out a way to package the summer heat upstairs and keep it for winter. As it was, we just looked forward to spring and fall.

A Central Pennsylvania summer day with high humidity can get pretty unbearable. Our upstairs "sauna" had to be well over 100 degrees on some days. But our Knickerbocker absolutely loved it! He'd lie on his back, belly up, feet in the air and there he would bake.

One memorable Saturday it was so hot that we knew there was absolutely no way we could spend the night in that bedroom. Since my parents happened to be away for the weekend, we took it upon ourselves to spend the night in their very pleasant air-conditioned home. We left our boy in his appointed place, roasting away. And we left the upstairs windows open in the hope that some air might blow through. Well blow it did. We were awakened in the middle of the night by a very violent thunderstorm—one of those where it seems to be pouring in all directions at once. Doug and I just looked at each other—"Nothing we can do about it now."

The next morning we went straight from my parents' house to church and then like it or not, we needed to return home to assess the damage. Unbelievably, we went upstairs to find only a bit of water on the carpet and the dresser at the one bedroom window. In the spare room directly across from our bedroom there was not one drop! We decided it was either a miracle or it had been so hot that the heat just evaporated the raindrops before they even had a chance to land. We were also surprised that Knick didn't fry a few brain cells. Then again...

Our furry friend was a good weather predictor though. We could be sitting in the living room on what seemed to be a beautiful summer day and all of a sudden, here he'd come. Belly fur scraping the ground, his entire body laid out flat in a kind of commando-crawl, Knick would come running through the kitchen, into the living room and behind the couch to his safe spot. Flattening himself in the stairwell proved a good hiding place as well. "Storm's coming," we'd say. Sure enough, the thunder and lightning would shortly follow. Oddly it seemed to be the lightning that scared him more than the thunder.

Unfortunately, weather wasn't the only thing that Knick was afraid of. As I've already mentioned, he had quite a reputation at the veterinary office. The first task was always to extricate him from his carrier. He had an amazing ability to remain stuck in there. Even when it was stood on end, perpendicular to the examination table, he would not slide out of that turquoise plastic cage for anything. We always had to take the top off and lift him out. From there, he'd immediately assume the position under my arm. Head stuck well beneath my armpit, our tiger tried with all his might to hide. Given his large hind end sticking out for all to see, this clearly proved futile.

Surprisingly, the vet techs absolutely loved him. They said they appreciated his attitude—and did he ever have one! Not only would the big fella hiss like a steam engine, he would also cry and scream like nobody's business. Even when they took the furball "to the back" for some sort of treatment, we could still hear him. We'd also hear much laughter and comments to the effect of, "Oh come on, we're not hurting you." Try telling him that!

As Knickie grew older, he had increased issues with constipation. The pharmacist thought it very comical when I gave him a prescription for a stool softener for my kitty. However, being middle-aged himself, he could sympathize with Knick. The worst times were the two occasions when the poor boy became so completely corked up that we had to take him for emergency treatment. As things go, both instances took place over a weekend, so we needed to drive him a half-hour away to the "Pet ER" rather than being able to go to his regular doctor.

After the initial examination, Knick would be whisked away for the "dig-out." It was a large facility and we could tell from the sound that he was a great distance away from where we were waiting in the exam room. But there was no mistaking that cry. It was him all right—but at a volume and pitch we had never heard before. Like a siren, the cry started out soft and low and then grew in intensity into a full-blown yell until it fully peaked and his cat breath was all used up. Then a few seconds later it would start again. If I hadn't known better, I would have thought it was a small child. I cannot even imagine how loud it must have been in that room with him. Interestingly, they made no mention of it when they returned him to us.

Now I certainly sympathized with Knick over the constipation issues and I can only imagine the sounds I might make if someone was digging me out without giving me anesthesia. But I've trimmed my fingernails and toenails plenty of times and not once have I cried. Not so with my kitty friend.

Knick had big, beautiful feet and toes and we couldn't bear the thought of having him declawed. There was really no reason for it as he learned to use a scratching post with minimal difficulty. Obviously, food was the perfect motivator for his training. In fact, he used his posts so vigorously that we were constantly needing to replace them. So at some point in his kittenhood, I began to clip the toenails of his front feet. As you can imagine, Knick was not very pleased about this. Nonetheless, he would come willingly every time I was ready to perform the dirty deed. Once he got older, and larger, it worked best for me to straddle him and actually almost sit on his back so that his front feet were directly in front of my knees. Not once in the hundreds of times that I clipped his nails, did I ever cut to the quick or cause him to bleed and to his credit, there were times that he was fine with his pedicure. On other occasions, he would scream like a banshee. *"MAAUUUUWWWW!!"* But ten toes later and a quick run to the food closet for a treat and all was forgiven.

My Story:

W ell who of us hasn't been afraid at one time or another? How many haven't cried or screamed or fussed over what seemed like a very trivial matter? Who among us has never overreacted to a situation? Our fears—large or small, actual or imagined, are very real to us. Because they're ours. And no one can, or should, tell us differently. Although it seemed silly to me for Knick to be afraid of lightning or toenail trimming, they were traumatic events in his cat mind. And who am I to judge?

As I mentioned earlier, I was terrified of public speaking. I still don't really like it but I've gotten more used to it. Thankfully, talking in front of a group of people ranks way up there on most everyone's fear list, so I get lots of support and empathy for my efforts. However for some people, being the center of attention is as natural as breathing; but talking to someone in a one-on-one conversation might scare them to death.

We all have our worries. I've known folks who are afraid of the seemingly most insignificant things. Or who go on and on about some situation that is highly traumatic for them. But for me, I just want to say, "Do you have a REAL problem you can tell me about?" I tend to judge others through my own lenses. If I can relate to what someone else is going through, I'm more sympathetic and understanding. But if their reaction to a situation or fear of something just seems irrational to me, I find it much more difficult to be supportive. Mercy is not high on my list of spiritual gifts.

What I need to remind myself of, is that God has created all of us uniquely. We all have different talents, gifts and abilities. Likewise, we all have different fears and issues that we struggle with. The key is to trust God in all of it.

When I gave that first message at church, I stood there a literal example of II Corinthians 12:9—"My strength is made perfect in weakness." (NKJV™) There is absolutely no way I could have stood up there and did that in my own strength or ability. I was having panic attacks a week before I did that first 5-minute offering. But what an awesome God we have who can take our weakest areas and use them for His glory! And it all comes back to obedience. If we are willing vessels, God will use all of us—the natural talents He gives us, plus the weak areas that He will make strong.

Now you might be thinking—I knew it! If I really give myself totally to God, He's going to make me do the thing I hate or fear the most. He's going to send me to deepest, darkest Africa—I'm sure of it! That's Doug's greatest fear. So far we haven't left Pennsylvania, so I think we're safe—for the moment anyway.

The truth is, when we're really on track with God, we'll go wherever He sends us and do whatever He tells us, because our greatest desire is to please Him. And that completely outweighs our greatest fear. So I could stand up there and give that first message—and all the ones that have followed—and I was and am okay—because I know I'm pleasing my Heavenly Father.

Like Knick, I've learned that when my Owner calls, I need to come running. Because whatever He has in store for me is for my own good. Whether I like it or not, whether it causes me fear or pain—even if it absolutely terrifies me—it is for my good. Or for the good of others. Every single time I called Knick, even if I needed to put him through some sort of medical ordeal, it was for his good. To do otherwise would have just been cruel. As hard as it was for me to watch him endure such pain, I knew it was necessary for his overall well-being. Every time I called, he came to me, even though he had no idea what it would mean for him. His coming could have resulted in pleasure, pain or fear. He didn't know which of those was in store for him on any given day. What he did know was that he could completely trust me. And he did. In the same way, we need to trust that in all things our Lord has good in mind for us.

I remember one instance when Doug and Knick crossed paths at about the same time and Knick went scurrying, apparently afraid that Doug hadn't seen him and was going to run into him. I said, "It's okay, your 'daddy' sees you. You're okay." Immediately, I heard a quiet voice in my mind—"You're okay. Your Daddy sees you." We were going through some very difficult situations at that time and fear was threatening to overwhelm me. But immediately after that I felt reassured.

Our Heavenly Daddy knows what's best for our overall well-being. Romans 8:28 says, "And we know that God causes everything to work together for the good of those who love God and are called according to His purpose for them." (NLT) We might not see those purposes immediately. We might not see them tomorrow or a month from now or even a year from now. We might not see them in our lifetimes. But that doesn't mean that verse isn't true. The purposes will be worked out in His timing and in His way. It's not up to us to worry about it or try to figure out how God should work or what He might ask of us if we make that deeper, more passionate commitment to Him. So we can't let our fears, whether real or imagined, stand in our way.

I also learned that God brings us along slowly. He knew that I would have completely fallen apart if He had shown me right from the start that I'd be standing up there giving an entire 30-minute sermon. He started with a 5-minute offering. He patiently and lovingly brought me along at my own pace and He continues to do so. Whether I cried or over-reacted or followed bravely, He has been there every step of the way. An offering, a message, 12 more messages, and now a book. Who knew? Only the One who created me, loved me and has gently guided me through every fear and scary ordeal I've ever endured.

Your Story:

What are you afraid of? Are your fears large or small? How do you react when scary situations threaten? Do you run and hope to hide from them? Or do you face them head on? Are you trusting in your own strength to work through your worries or are you placing your faith in Someone much greater and stronger than you'll ever be?

When Joshua assumed leadership of the Israelites after Moses had died, the Lord told him over and over again to "be strong and courageous." I'm guessing that the reason God told him again and again was because Joshua wasn't feeling very strong or courageous.

Have you ever been in a situation that you absolutely knew you couldn't handle on your own? How did you react? Did you try to accomplish the task in your own strength anyway? Or did you place your hope and trust in the One who could help you to be brave in the face of fear, danger or pain?

If you have never had an experience of God's strength being made perfect in weakness, I wonder if perhaps you've never had to trust Him to do something that you could never do in your own strength. I'm not necessarily suggesting that you go searching for one of these opportunities. But if and when one comes your way, don't scurry to hide behind the couch or cower on the stairs. Let it be an occasion to stretch and grow your faith in ways that you may have never dreamed were possible. Take the risk to see how it feels to accomplish something beyond your own capabilities.

Also recognize that in most cases, you'll need to take that first step of obedience when your fears are at their greatest height. When Joshua needed to lead the Israelites across the Jordan River, the water was at flood stage. Talk about a fearful situation! It wasn't until the priests actually stepped into the water, that the torrent stopped flowing. Sure enough, it walled up just as the Red Sea had when Moses led the people across it. But if the priests had not been brave enough to take that first step, they never would have experienced God's miraculous work.

If you're facing circumstances that seem insurmountable, know that the High Priest has already gone before you. Jesus has already made the way for you to be able to navigate even the most fearful of situations and eventually come through on dry ground. That's not to say that you won't have to pass through the water; but when you are brave enough to take that first step, He'll do the rest.

Being strong and courageous in the face of one of your greatest fears and knowing that the strength and courage is not your own, is the most awesome feeling you'll ever know. But the only way you'll know it is to face your fears to begin with.

So come running when your Owner calls. Trust that your Lord has only the best in store for you. Rejoice when your response to Him results in pleasure. Be brave when you are called to a situation that brings you fear or pain. Know that you can hide under His strong arm when you're too afraid to look. And in all things, rest in the knowledge that God's love for you is enough. Your Daddy sees you. And He always has only the best in mind for you.

Chapter 5

He was uncoordinated...
See your inner beauty

Knick's Story:

Cats have such a reputation for being graceful, dexterous, agile creatures. Not so our sweet Knick. I do believe his size and weight issues contributed to his lack of physical prowess, but even during his slimmer years, any hint of athleticism simply eluded him. This was proven at a fairly young age when Doug felt the need to test the old adage, "A cat always lands on his feet." Holding the boy upside-down high above the sofa, my dear husband suddenly let him go. Poor Knick dropped like a stone, landing on his back, stunned and confused on the couch below. Regaining his footing, he gave a confused look and wandered off. I, of course, was livid. "What were you doing?!"

"I thought they're always supposed to land on their feet. I just wanted to try it with him." Perhaps given a higher altitude to work with, Knick might have made the turn, but I'm not so sure. Physical skills were just not in his blood.

However, he would manage to jump up on our kitchen counters on a regular basis. Anytime the hefty tabby could find something to taste-test, he was there. If there was no actual food to sample, dirty dishes to lick suited him just as well. Many a night we were awakened by the sound of silverware dropping into the stainless steel sink. This would be followed by a loud cry of "KNICK! Get down!!!" In response, a loud thud would shortly be heard. We thought for sure that one of those times, 18 pounds of cat would go straight through the softwood floors and down into the basement.

Jumping for Knick was more like a leap of faith followed by a mad scramble to get a foothold on whatever surface he was trying to reach. For unknown reasons, the large fellow liked to go to the top of the recliner and then jump down into the very small space behind it in the corner of the living room. After he had done whatever it was he did back there, of course he needed to get out. And the only way out was up. Front feet clamoring and claws scraping, he'd try to get enough of a grip to scale his way out. Usually after five or six tries, a striped tabby head would finally appear followed by the rest of his weary body.

Another jumping opportunity came during one of Knick's occasional outdoor adventures. On this particular day, he decided that it would be interesting to see what lay beyond the boundaries of the fenced-in deck. In a single bound, he leapt from the deck to the covered hot tub. Obviously that didn't get him high enough to survey the outside world. So he took another leap to the top of the wooden fence—and promptly tumbled completely over the top and out of sight.

Racing around to the other side, I found a somewhat stunned kitty standing in the grass. To his credit, I do believe he landed on his feet. With a sympathetic heart, I scooped up my sweet boy and back inside we went, leaving such daring pursuits for another day.

I would be remiss to leave out that Knick did have one shining moment of athletic skill, although it ended in a most unfortunate way. At the end of our living room was a window that opened up into the back room of the house and our computer table was immediately below the window. Sometimes we would open the window in order to allow some heat to travel from the living room into the unheated "office." On one such day, a certain furry teenager decided to test his wings.

Running at full speed through the living room, he leapt to the windowsill and onto the computer table, jumped down, went through the mud room, into the kitchen and back to the living room where he repeated the sequence. Lap after lap he made, while Doug and I relaxed on the couch, enjoying the circular event. After ten laps or so, I made the executive decision that it was time to close the window. Knick was on the computer table at the time watching intently as I lowered the glass pane and then fastened the wooden shutters.

Shortly thereafter we heard him coming through the kitchen and the dining room area. When he got to the archway opening into the living room, something in his fuzzy cat mind must have kicked in and he once again took off running. Like a gazelle he went, racing the length of the room, jumping at just the right moment—and slamming his head straight into the closed shutters. Bouncing off, he landed on his backside. With a shake of the head and a bit dazed from the unexpected blow, our sweet one wandered off, leaving us alone in our snickering.

One of Knickie's favorite activities was lying on the table in front of the windows in the back room where he could fully enjoy the warmth of the afternoon sunshine. Especially in his later years, he really appreciated the "helper-chair" that we placed next to the table. It enabled him to reach his destination much more easily. Getting there was one thing. Staying there was something else altogether. Knick had the ill-fated habit of lying extremely close to the edge of the table. And once he entered the peaceful state of REM sleep, one false move was all it took for Mr. Grace to pitch right over the side and land on the carpet-covered concrete below. More than once he fell from his perch, but that never stopped him from taking his assumed position the next time. Maybe he just enjoyed living on the edge.

Another route to his favorite snoozing spot was through the living room window and then along the computer table until he reached the end where he could make the one foot step across to his table. I happened to be sitting at the PC one day when my fuzzy friend came ambling by. During the last leg of his journey past the printer, suddenly he lost his stability and nearly slipped off the edge. Stunned, he quickly spread out all four paws to brace himself and recover his balance. With a spin of his head, he shot me an embarrassed look. *"You didn't see that, did you?"*

"No, Knickie, I didn't see a thing."

Jumping and balance were not Knick's only physical struggles. His spatial-relational skills were lacking as well. Our tiger-striped boy had one of the largest litter boxes known to mankind. Nevertheless, consistently getting his waste <u>inside</u> the plastic tub was another matter. One of the problems was that he would dutifully dig his hole—and then sit right in the middle of the crater. This often resulted in his hind end hanging over the edge of the box with his solid waste dropping on the newspaper below. When he did manage to position himself so his toileting results ended up where they were supposed to—the boy had no proficiency in covering it up. Digging furiously at the pit he was sitting in just resulted in a larger hole while the offending material remained exposed at the top of the heap. Another clever, yet equally unsuccessful technique was to paw frantically at the newsprint outside of the box, turning to look after every three or four scrapes to see what progress was being made. Usually after fifteen seconds or so of effort, he'd give one last passing glance—*"Oh heck with it—that's good enough!"*—and away he'd stroll.

One very rare exception to this "unable to hit the side of a barn" concept happened once—and only once! As Sunday afternoons go in the Tingen household, we were all down for our respective naps—I on the bed upstairs, Doug on the couch, and Knick wherever he chose to be. Awakening from my snooze, I wandered downstairs to find that my beloved buddy was not within my immediate sight. Then I noticed the closed door. It must have been winter and "someone" had closed off the mud room door to keep the cold air from filtering into the kitchen area.

Opening the door and going into the computer room, I immediately found who I was looking for. But from the offending stench, I knew that there was more to see than a "relieved to be rescued" cat. Taking a few tentative steps into the room, I saw the most astonishing sight ever. There was one of Doug's dress shoes—and in the place where only a foot should go—was the largest pile of you know what. Not one single piece was outside of that shoe! How Knick ever managed to position himself over that small cavity and completely fill the hole is a mystery that remains to this day. Needless to say, my hysterical laughter aroused my still sleeping spouse. Also needless to say, he was not nearly so amused as I. But that was certainly the final time he left Knick penned up in a room, with or without shoes.

My Story:

L ike it or not, I have to admit that I have a few things in common with Knick as far as coordination goes. I wouldn't say I'm completely inept as far as athleticism, but when it comes to perceptual and spatial-relationship abilities, I certainly have my share of struggles. Doug puts it in more simple terms—"You have no concept of where your body is in space." All I know is that it hurts. I can be walking through a doorway and suddenly it's like the doorframe itself jumps out and slams itself into my shoulder. Or I'll innocently reach up to open a kitchen cabinet and when I get within about two inches of the cupboard, out of nowhere, the velocity of my hand's movement will increase to warp speed and my fist will slam into the door—for no apparent reason.

Thankfully, God blessed me with a strong body because for all my bruises, not once have I ever broken a bone. I'm also grateful that He gave me an extremely hard head. There are times I've wondered if I shouldn't just wear a helmet.

One of those occasions happened over twenty years ago shortly after Doug and I were married. We were at our friend's house and I was challenging him in a game of Ping-Pong. Being quite skilled athletically and also extremely competitive, Steve was more than frustrated that I was beating him in the game. We were in his basement, which had a low ceiling and even lower ductwork with which I was about to become quite familiar. Not even realizing it was there, I ran for a shot—and slammed my head straight into the ductwork. The force knocked me on my butt, but I somehow immediately bounced back up.

Though it wasn't the last, I believe that might have been the first time I learned that if you hit your head hard enough, you really do see stars! After a few minutes of clearing out the cobwebs, we decided to resume the game. I can be quite competitive myself and was not about to let a blow to the skull interfere with my impending victory. Steve, on the other hand, was devastated, to put it mildly, when I still went on to claim the win. Doug, my concussion, and I went straight home after that, never to play another game of table tennis in that basement again.

So what does any of this have to do with spiritual things? In 1 Samuel 16:7, it says, "The Lord does not look at the things man looks at. Man looks at the outward appearance, but the Lord looks at the heart." (NIV)

We so quickly judge each other by external characteristics—physical appearance, athletic skill, manual abilities. But our Lord looks past all of that and goes straight to the soul. He cares much more about the state of our spiritual selves than he does our physical bodies. Once again, this is clearly stated in Scripture. "Spend your time and energy in training yourself for spiritual fitness. Physical exercise has some value, but spiritual exercise is much more important, for it promises a reward in both this life and the next." (1 Timothy 4:7b-8, NLT)

For the past several years, Doug and I have renewed our efforts to become more physically fit—which seems to take on more importance as you hit the mid-life stage. So at this point, I'm probably in the best shape of my life and I'm quite pleased about that. However, I'm also learning that as wonderful as that is, I cannot neglect my spiritual side. God clearly showed this to me one Saturday during a prayer seminar at our church.

I was feeling kind of stale in my prayer life and knew that in part, it was because I was spending more concentrated, focused periods of time on physical exercise than I was on spiritual pursuits. So I thought the mini-retreat might be very beneficial.

During one of the prayer exercises, God showed me a picture in my mind's eye of an overflowing fountain. He showed me that if I continue to drink His life-giving water, then His Spirit would well up and overflow in me. It will bring me life, so that I in turn can bring life to others as the water flows out into small streams that break up and go out in every direction.

During a later exercise, He expanded upon this concept. I took a seat by a small rock fountain during our personal reflection time. While contemplating the flow of the water, I removed a stone from the fountain and held it in my hands, feeling the moisture. Very shortly I noticed that the stone had dried out—and so had my hand. I realized that when we're not in the flow of God's stream, we very quickly dry out. And we dry out those around us as well. Looking at the pebble, I also noticed how dull and lifeless it now looked. So I put it back with its friends and watched as it became renewed and refreshed as the water flowed over it once more. How rapidly the stone became shiny again!

Then I noticed that the way I had positioned the stone, the light reflected off of it just so, that it created a beautiful star shape, shining brightly in the corner of the now wet pebble. And God brought to mind my favorite Scripture verse. "Do everything without complaining or arguing, so that you may become blameless and pure, children of God without fault in a crooked and depraved generation, in which you shine like stars in the universe as you hold out the word of life—in order that I may boast on the day of Christ that I did not run or labor for nothing." (Philippians 2:14-16, NIV)

The Lord had previously impressed upon me that I could shine for Him, but this time I saw it in a clearer way. I need to stay in His flow of life-giving water in order to shine. If I neglect my spiritual growth, I'm not only hurting myself—I'm also hindering others. It was a beautiful picture and a poignant reminder to me of the necessity for me to keep my priorities in perspective.

Knick may not have had a lot of physical skills, but he more than made up for it with his spirit. He loved me with all his heart and his sweet, constant presence was there for me through some of the most difficult times of my life. May I too be more concerned with the state of my heart rather than my body, that I may shine brightly as God's Spirit flows through me and brings hope and life to all those around me.

Your Story:

Like Knick and me, maybe you're not the most coordinated, athletic or physically talented. Maybe you don't feel like you're very smart or outwardly attractive. Perhaps you were always the last one selected when teams were chosen. Could be you were constantly teased by the other kids. If so, maybe it's time to find a new perspective. Recognize anew the power and strength and life that can only come from the inside. Consider the worth that Jesus sees in you—not from your natural, physical talents, but from your heart.

The Bible tells us this in 1 Corinthians 1:26-29. "Remember, dear brothers and sisters, that few of you were wise in the world's eyes, or powerful, or wealthy when God called you. Instead, God deliberately chose things the world considers foolish in order to shame those who think they are wise. And He chose those who are powerless to shame those who are powerful. God chose things despised by the world, things counted as nothing at all, and used them to bring to nothing what the world considers important, so that no one can ever boast in the presence of God." (NLT) Scripture also teaches that the last will be first and the first will be last.

God LOVES the underdog! How many times do we hear of a true story or see a fact-based movie where the most unlikely of persons becomes the hero? Or the sports team that has been a complete failure somehow pulls out the most unbelievable victory imaginable? I don't know about you, but I love those types of stories! They remind us over and over again, that anything is possible. Especially when we let God be the source of our strength.

This world places so much emphasis on physical beauty. We're bombarded with it constantly on commercials, in advertisements, in magazines, on billboards. Young girls are starving themselves because society tells them they're worthless if they're not thin enough. But scripture says this to women. "Don't be concerned about the outward beauty that depends on fancy hairstyles, expensive jewelry, or beautiful clothes. You should be known for the beauty that comes from within, the unfading beauty of a gentle and quiet spirit, which is so precious to God." (1 Peter 3:3-4, NLT)

God is not concerned with our outward appearances. In fact, did you know that Jesus himself was probably quite homely? In Isaiah, there are some prophetic words given about Jesus and Isaiah 53:2 says this. "There was nothing beautiful or majestic about his appearance, nothing to attract us to him." (NLT)

Now think about that for a minute. Our looks are pretty much a result of genetics; we don't have any say over what we look like when we're born. But Jesus had a choice! He made the decision to somehow, miraculously, transform Himself from God into a baby, born to Mary. But He was God! So if He was going to stuff His God-self into a human body, don't you think He would have at least made himself good-looking? Wouldn't it have made sense for Jesus—the only perfect, sinless human being ever to live—to have the perfect body and the most handsome face? If physical appearances were important, shouldn't Jesus have been the most attractive person ever to walk the face of the earth? But He wasn't. Yet He was the greatest leader that ever lived.

How often are we prone to following someone or wanting to be like him or her because we're attracted to their physical appearance? The followers of Jesus weren't attracted to Him because of His looks; they followed Him because of who He was on the inside—and because of the love that spilled out from Him to everyone He met.

So let your love and your spirit and your heart flow out to others. Stay in God's life-giving stream. Let His love shine through you so you can hold out the hope of life to others. And if you stumble now and then? Regain your balance as quickly as possible and keep going. It worked for Knick—and it'll work for you too.

Chapter 6

He was domesticated...
Accept yourself as you are

Knick's Story:

A s you've likely figured out by now, Knickerbocker was not one of those cats who was longing to get outdoors and catch a fieldmouse for dinner. I don't think he'd have lasted the night if he had somehow ended up outside. Especially in winter—my gosh—how would he have ever survived without his heat vent? No, Knick would have been repulsed by the idea of having to kill his own food. In fact, we believe that if given a choice, he would have preferred to sit at the table and use silverware. Eating with his face just didn't seem refined enough for our boy. (You can also see that both Doug and Knick had immaculate table manners and knew just when to smile for the camera.)

On one memorable occasion, our tabby proved without a shadow of a doubt just what kind of hunter he was. I was awakened by a horrific caterwauling. I had no idea what it was, but I hustled downstairs to look. In the mud room I discovered a very small gray mouse. I had absolutely no idea that mice could yell, but other than the huge and for once silent feline off to his left, there was no one else around. By this time I had called for Doug to join me. Sometime during the commotion, the little creature scurried off into the computer room so we quickly shut the door. Knick was standing in the mud room with us looking bewildered. With a voice of triumph, Doug picked him up, opened the door and tossed him into the room, shouting encouragement as he went. "Knick—here you go—this is your big moment—go get the mouse!" After several moments of complete silence, we curiously opened the door. There he was—18 pounds of fear standing on the table with a look on his face that said, *"Hey—will someone take care of this already?"* Seeing his opportunity for escape, the little creature scurried off towards the kitchen. Our disappointment instantly dissolved into laughter.

During another of our outside deck adventures, Knickie encountered a different form of wildlife. He spotted the tiniest bug imaginable crawling along one of the wooden planks. Getting as close as possible without touching it, he must have taken a good sniff—and then promptly opened his mouth wide, stuck out his tongue and gagged. Complete with the *"Aack"* sound, of course! Once again, I just shook my head and laughed out loud. After that my feline friend stayed with safer activities like lying on his side and sunning himself. No predator/prey games for our kitty.

Our Knick also seemed to be quite sensitive as far as his little padded tootsies went. He very much preferred a soft, sand-like litter to a more course texture. And wouldn't you know it—every time I found one that seemed to suit him just perfectly—the brand would be discontinued and I'd have to start my search all over again.

Grass is soft so you would think that would have felt nice to him, but the few rare times he ended up in the lawn, it was quickly evident that he was not a fan. Lifting one paw in the air at a time and shaking it, one after another, he crept along, more than happy to be rescued from the foreign green material and returned to a more familiar environment. Just for fun, we also let him out on the deck one time after a major snowstorm. No surprise there—Knick was not very fond of snow and ice on his tender toes either.

One area that our boy definitely excelled in was with his grooming. After a full bath, that striped fur was soft as silk! Although I must admit, "Chinchilla Knick" wasn't real thrilled about cleaning his backside—and I will certainly agree that "licking your butt" is just plain gross. One of the few times we did spy the tabby giving himself a thorough cleansing was right before an Elder from my childhood church was going to be making a visit. Somehow he knew.

There was one notable exception to Knickie's bathing routine. He absolutely refused to wash himself when we were on vacation, assumedly due to being upset and depressed. If you've ever petted a cat that hasn't bathed for an entire week, it's not a pleasant feel. But without fail, within an hour of our arrival home, his chinchilla fur would be back to its full glory.

No, our Knick was not a wild-at-heart male by any means. One summer evening, a cat of the female persuasion happened by and apparently was quite interested in our tabby. He was at his usual spot in the computer room and although Knick was many years post-"operation," this girl somehow knew our big boy was there. After getting no response to her plaintive cries, she suddenly jumped at the screen of the open window. Heart racing and pulse quickening, Knickie beat a hasty retreat to the security of the living room, again with that disconcerted look that only he could give—*"Yikes—what was that all about?"* Meanwhile, the faint outline of a rebuffed feline remained indented in the screen.

My Story:

Knick just didn't quite fit the stereotypical picture of how a large, male tabby should behave. Or any cat for that matter. His outward characteristics said one thing, but his personality and actions said quite another. Still, he was very comfortable in his own skin. He had no problem being Knickerbocker. That was simply who he was – take it or leave it. *"If you're looking for a good mouser, you might want to bring someone else in, because I'm going to be over here cowering on the table until you dispose of the rodent, okay?"* Knick could not have killed any sort of critter if his life had depended on it, and Doug and I were perfectly fine with that. We adored Knick for who he was and we never put expectations on him that he wasn't able to fulfill. We loved his uniqueness and the fact that he was a cat only in his fur.

Shouldn't we all be accepted for who we are? Can't we be loved simply for being ourselves? Shouldn't we feel free to be who we were created to be rather than trying to fulfill others' expectations? I am so very thankful that we have a God who does just that. Our Lord loves us just the way we are—and for who we are—and not because of anything we've done. God loves me just because I'm Patti. I don't have to do anything more to earn His love, and I certainly don't have to try to be someone I'm not.

One thing I'm not is a mother. At least not a biological one. To my surprise, I've ended up being a spiritual mother to a number of folks, but that has been all from God. On my own, I've just never had any drive for parenthood. Babies are fine, don't get me wrong, but if you put an infant in front of me, and there's also a puppy or a kitten within sight—sorry, but I'm going for the pet every time. As a child, I always played with stuffed animals and very rarely with dolls. And babysitting? I think one time I stayed with my younger cousin for an evening and she needed some help with a bit of toileting. Let's just say that Knick and I have a similar gag reflex: "Aack!"

I am so thankful for family and friends and most importantly a very sweet and understanding husband who have graciously accepted that giving birth was just not something I had any interest in. I'd judge myself now and then, especially early in our marriage—and wonder what was wrong with me that I didn't have any motherly longings. But when I stopped the wondering, I discovered I was at peace with it—so I decided to stop wondering. As a result, I was better able to grow into the person God had made me to be.

I'm very grateful that our church has a strong belief in people serving in their areas of giftedness rather than forcing folks into more traditional, stereotypical roles based on age or gender or some other outward characteristic. By now you could probably guess how well I'd do at serving in the nursery. I don't even want to think about that!

We don't need to do or be something we're not. Yet far too often we try to be. Or we expect others to do or be something they are not. My poor husband! I grew up in a very traditional household as far as gender roles go. My Dad takes care of house maintenance, the cars and the yardwork. My Mom is in charge of cooking, cleaning and laundry. That arrangement works perfectly for them. In large part this is due to both of them being very skilled at the areas in which they are in charge.

So when we got married, I naturally assumed that things would work in a similar manner. I knew Doug would change the oil in the cars—both cars—every 3,000 miles. There was only one problem. Doug had very little mechanical ability—and even less skill at oil changing. I figured he'd get better at it as he went along. He didn't. Time after time he made the effort—and every now and then things went very smoothly and quickly—it seemed like a breakthrough! But 3,000 miles later, or maybe 5,000 since of course he'd put it off, it would be back to square one. I'd look outside and see the writhing legs sticking out from underneath the vehicle and I knew it was bad. "Righty tighty, lefty loosey, *&%#$!!"

My sweet spouse tried to change the oil in our cars for over ten years! Bless his heart. He was simply trying to please me and be the man that he knew I wanted him to be. Despite seeing his struggles over and over again, I continued with the mindset of traditional male/female stereotypes and didn't allow my brain to consider any other options. Then one day I experienced something like a revelation from Heaven. I said, "Hey—you know what? We could just take the cars to one of those oil changing places—and they could do it there!" Doug looked at me in stunned amazement and, to his great credit, simply responded, "Yes, we could."

Since that time our marriage has become much more balanced. I take care of cleaning, ironing and yardwork. Doug does grocery shopping, laundry and most of the cooking. And the mechanic a few blocks away takes care of the cars. We're all much happier—the mechanic included. Doug and I both greatly enjoy watching sports on TV, but we had to chuckle the day I was watching Purdue vs. Michigan after coming in from mowing the lawn and Doug was in the kitchen making a large pot of soup. It's so good to be able to be yourself!

We have many friends who, like Knick, are also comfortable in their own skin. One great example is a gentleman who Doug worked for at one time. John owns a business selling various types of turf equipment, manure spreaders, etc. and he is very mechanically inclined. He's also a great dancer. His business is housed in an old warehouse, which has beautiful wood floors—just perfect for dancing. So during a break one day, John's teacher came to his workplace and he took his tap lesson. Doug said it was so humorous to hear his boss on the phone making a business transaction in one moment, and an instant later to hear, "tappety, tappety, tappety, tappety, tap" as John made his way down the hallway for his lesson. What a great example of someone who is free to be himself.

Not only am I appreciative of family, friends and a God who loves me just as I am—I am also extremely grateful for a church that believes that as well. One of the comments we hear over and over again from people who walk into our fellowship for the first time is, "This place is so real. There is such a freedom here just to be myself. I don't feel like anyone's putting any expectations on me to look or dress or talk a certain way in order to fit in." That concept is also captured in our identity statement—"Breaking rules, breaking barriers, breaking chains." We might not always look or act the way tradition would say a church should. But we're not following tradition. We're following Jesus—and He more than anyone who ever lived knew how to break rules, barriers, and chains. My goodness— touching lepers, associating with prostitutes, eating with sinners. How dare He?

How dare WE! How dare we politely sit someone in the back pew who might not smell the best. How self-righteous when we cast disparaging looks at a person who isn't dressed well enough to fit the culture of the rest of the group. How cruel to talk to the parents rather than the child who is in a wheelchair because we can't see past his or her disability. Matthew 25:40 says, "I tell you the truth, whatever you did for one of the least of these brothers of mine, you did for Me." (NIV)

Our church is full of "the least of these." We have many who don't quite measure up on the outside—outcasts by the world's standards. But they are welcomed with open arms and huge smiles— as is anyone who steps foot on our property. We will love and accept anyone who walks through our doors regardless of whether or not he or she has the appearance of a good, upstanding, righteous churchgoer. Who are those people anyway? How do we know who they really are or what they're like on the inside? Why do we so quickly judge by appearances—and think we're right?

After all, by all outward indications, Knick was a cat.

Your Story:

How about you? Do you feel free to be yourself? Are you comfortable in your own skin? Or are you trying in vain to do or be something or someone you're not in order to please somebody else? Do you have people in your life who love you exactly the way you are? Or are you constantly struggling for acceptance?

Whether in your workplace, home, or church, are you working or serving in areas in which you excel? Or are you laboring in frustration because you or someone else thinks a task "ought" to be yours to complete? Do you feel pressured by unspoken rules of how things should be done? The Bible likens the functions of the members of a church to the physical body. When healthy, our mortal bodies work in perfect harmony because each part of the body knows and performs its role the way it was designed to. In the same way, the church is to function with each person giving or serving in the area in which he or she is gifted.

It seems so obvious, yet I know this is a struggle for many individuals and churches. Too often, Christians get the idea that helping out in some area of ministry needs to be laborious and full of drudgery. Years ago, our drama team did a skit one Sunday morning where one of the characters said something like, "If you're not miserable in serving, it doesn't count." I'm not sure where that false idea came from, but we're quick to believe it. It's almost like somewhere along the way the church got the idea that in order to earn riches for Heaven we need to be miserable during our life on earth. That's NOT what God has called us to! And what a horrible example we give to the world with that type of mindset. When you're serving in the areas in which you are gifted, your service will bring fulfilling life to yourself and to those around you.

Moving beyond yourself, how are you treating others? Are you willing to let your spouse, or parent, or boss, be who he or she is? Or do you project unrealistic expectations in the hope that one day someone will finally measure up? Are you judging by outward appearances only? Or are you inclined to look a bit deeper and see who those people really are beneath their outer coats?

Far too often we underestimate God's grace—both for ourselves and for others. We have a merciful God. The Lord understands our struggles and our weaknesses. He knows that life is hard and that it beats us up. Let's not make it even harder by beating others or ourselves up simply because they or we don't measure up to certain standards. Judging is so much easier than loving. Maybe that's why we accomplish it so much more readily. Let's try setting a new standard—not a standard of judgment but one of love. A love that embraces without criticizing, that gives without expectations, that welcomes without prejudice. Let's look beyond our own agendas and our own needs long enough to see a hurting friend, neighbor or family member who might be longing for acceptance. Give those people the gift of love and encouragement that they deserve simply for being themselves, no matter what their "outer cat" may indicate.

Chapter 7

He was funny...
Learn to laugh often

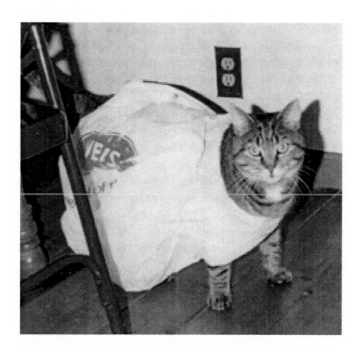

Knick's Story:

We were never at a loss for laughs with Knick around. He was quite a character. As you know, the boy had this thing about plastic grocery bags. Not only did he get much pleasure out of licking them—but as you can see, he also greatly enjoyed wearing them. At first I thought maybe it was just an accident—that he had somehow gotten tangled up in the bag post-lick. But no—it seemed to be with purpose that our tiger would work to get his large cranium through the handle of a bag and then wear it like a cape. Upon dressing, "Supercat" was ready to fight kitty crime anywhere in the tri-state area.

Once adorned, Knickie was quite content to model the latest in grocery store fashion for quite some time. He'd amble through the house or perhaps have a bite to eat—assuming it happened to be feeding time. One time he even ventured upstairs and jumped up on the bed for a midday nap—plastic and all. Eventually, he'd work both of his front legs through the opening as the sack continued on its journey over his body. Often the bag would become quite taut around his portly mid-section so I'd stay within rescue distance in case the plastic threatened to cut off his belly circulation. Eventually his hind feet and tail would come through as well and the cape would fall off to complete the undressing. At that point he would usually cast a casual glance back as if to say, *"What was that?"* and continue on with his day, leaving the now useless bag in his wake.

Usually, "Big Knick", as we were fond of calling him, was satisfied with just wearing one bag and that would be it for that adventure. However, on one memorable day, he felt the need to branch out from his usual practice. We had the closet door open and Knick made his way over to explore. I wasn't really paying attention and didn't look until my ears heard the sound of plastic rustling—lots of plastic. There he was—huge tabby head through the handle of one bag—one bag stuffed full of at least twenty others. Christmas had arrived early that year and "Santa-cat" was making his rounds. *"Step—step—rustle...step—step—rustle..."* After every few footsteps he'd glance back with a questioning look as to what was making the offending sound. He also wore quite a look of weariness as if to say, *"Oh, what a heavy burden I bear."* But he carried on gamely, because—hey—someone had to do it. Like a good mom, I laughed and promptly took a picture.

Knickerbocker provided us with comic relief throughout his lifetime. As a youngster, he had his share of the usual kittenish humor. One of his favorite games was to strategically place one little forepaw down the knothole in one of the kitchen floorboards, and then spin his body around in a tight circle like Curly from "The 3 Stooges." The only thing missing was the "whoop, whoop, whoop" sound.

As Knick aged, his sense of humor became more sophisticated. Like many other mysteries in the life of Knick, he loved to lay on top of cardboard boxes, like a shirt box. He wouldn't lie IN the box; he liked it with the lid on, smashed down just so, in order to perfectly fit his striped frame. We had to make sure that every Christmas at least someone in the family received some sort of present that came with a box so Knick would have a fresh resting place for the new year. So much for the expensive fleece bed I bought him.

One lazy Saturday afternoon, we Tingen's were all in the living room. I was relaxing on the couch, Doug was lying on the floor reading, and Knickie was settling onto his box. There was only one thing disturbing us. Well, two of us anyway. Unbeknownst to him, Doug was quite annoyingly drumming his fingers on the wooden floorboard beneath his hand. From my vantage point on the sofa, I was able to survey the entire scene. Knick was trying his best to relax but he kept gazing over at Doug with quite a sense of irritation. I knew exactly how he felt because I was equally irked but was trying my best to just let Doug be Doug. (See last chapter on letting people be themselves.) In my mind I repeated my mantra over and over again, "Don't say anything, don't say anything, don't say anything..." And then I saw him—my hero.

With one last look of desperation, he leapt off his box like he had been shot out of a cannon. *"Budda, budda, budda, budda, budda, budda, BOOF!"* Knick's front paws pounced on top of Doug's hands in a motion that clearly said, *"STOP IT!!!"* Then he straightened back up, turned tail, and <u>strode</u> back to his box. Making one spin, he positioned himself in a perfect circle, heaved a huge sigh and closed his eyes. *"<u>Now</u> a cat can get some rest!"* Doug was still recovering from his state of shock as it obviously scared him to death. I, of course, was abounding in laughter, having literally rolled off the couch.

On another occasion it was Knick who got the scare and I was privileged to watch that unfold as well. Our feline was quite territorial and he saw to it that every single thing in our home was labeled as belonging to Knickerbocker. Whether it was a piece of furniture or the smallest knick-knack, the kitty did his duty in marking it up as quickly as possible. (Speaking of knick-knacks, we always joked that had I gotten his brother we could have had Knick-Knack. Actually, we could have had the whole rhyme—"Knick-Knack, Patti-whack, give a Doug a bone.") But I digress.

On a visit with my Grandmother one day, she gave me a cute little country-type doll that fit perfectly with our décor. She stood about a foot high and I decided she would look nice on the bathroom floor beside a basket. So there she stood just inside the door. It just so happened that I was still in the bathroom when a certain cat was making his way there as well. Knowing that he had not yet seen her, I eagerly awaited Knick's shock. Sure enough, he rounded that corner and was eye to eye with the little girl. Sucking wind, he drew his head back as his golden eyes grew even larger than usual. After making his recovery and cautiously checking her out, he gave her the official Knick seal of approval and marked her up as worthy of joining the family.

Our little family was never short on hilarity—even when some of us were sleeping. I was preparing to go out one evening and wanted to ask Doug something before I left. He happened to be napping upstairs on the loveseat in our spare room. I decided to disturb him anyway. Also napping was "you know who"—lying on the carpet next to the loveseat in an almost identical position. Both were rolled kind of onto their backs facing in the same direction. And both were sound asleep. "Doug, Doug, DOUG!" Finally I was loud enough to get a response—actually 2 responses. In immediate succession and with identical sleepy expressions and slight turns of their heads, I heard, "Huh?" *"Mauw?"* "Oh forget it," I responded, as I giggled and went on my way.

My boys were again in perfect synchronization one night—in the middle of the night. Now Knick could snore with the best of them. He probably could have been diagnosed with sleep apnea. Seriously, you could hear him snoring from across the room. On this particular evening I awoke to a symphony of snorts—in perfect rhythm. *"Zzzzzz"…"Zzzzzz" … "Zzzzzz"…"Zzzzzz"* "How am I supposed to get any sleep?" I asked out loud as I sat up in bed. Well if you can't beat em, might as well join em. So for a few rounds I jumped in with my own snoring sound just for fun, as there was an opening in the cadence. Then I chuckled softly to myself and lay back down, drifting off to sleep in the heart-warming presence of my two best friends.

My Story:

I don't know about you, but I love to laugh. Growing up in a household that was full of joking and fun, I knew that anyone I married would need to have a great sense of humor as well. Doug has a number of wonderful qualities, but his ability to routinely keep me in stitches is definitely one of the things that drew me to him. My knees have buckled on numerous occasions when he's dropped a hilarious line at just the right moment. One evening we had a friend over for dinner. He had been battling depression and we thought he could use a night just to have a few laughs. And laugh we did! The next Sunday at church he told another friend, "You wouldn't know it just to look at him, but Doug is really funny." That statement gave us yet one more memory to put in our "laughter bank".

Doug and I will recall humorous stories on a regular basis. We have a whole collection of things that have happened to other people or us over the years that absolutely crack us up. So we'll re-tell the stories to each other over and over and over again—and we laugh just as much or more than when it happened for the first time. And over time we just keep adding to our collection.

The Bible reinforces the importance of humor as well. Proverbs 17:22 says, "A cheerful heart is good medicine, but a broken spirit saps a person's strength." (NLT) The King James Version says,

"A merry heart doeth good like a medicine but a broken spirit dries up the bones."

I've always thought my paternal Grandmother was a great example of this verse. She passed away at the age of 96 and she was in pretty good health and laughing up until the last few months of her life.

My Grandma laughed—all the time. It was just a natural part of her personality. I remember when Doug and I first got married. He's from northwestern PA so he was not accustomed to the Pennsylvania Dutch way of speaking, which is prevalent in Lancaster County. So we'd visit my grandparents and they'd both be talking—at the same time—each telling a different story—with strong Dutch accents, using words and phrases he had never heard before. Obviously, he was rather unnerved by this. He said, "What do I do? I don't know what they're talking about." I told him, "It's okay. You don't have to know. Just sit there and laugh. You'll be fine." And he was.

If we leave out the laughter, fun and lightheartedness, I think we leave out a part of life that God intended for us to enjoy. We're also missing out on part of His creation. If God created us, and He did, with all our different feelings and emotions, then God also invented our sense of humor. And I believe God loves a good laugh.

A number of years ago, I gave a message at church entitled, "God's More Fun Than You Might Think". When I first got the idea for the message, I thought, "This is going to be great!" because God had given me some humorous things to say when I had spoken before. In fact, Doug said at one point, "You're not that funny in real life. You get up there, you're like Lucille Ball." So I thought, "Wow—a whole message on humor—they'll be rolling in the aisles." So with pen and paper in hand, I pronounced, "Okay God—I'm ready. Let it rip!" Well, do you think I could come up with even one amusing story? "Sure, tell me to do a message on humor and then don't give me anything funny to say." Then I thought, "That's pretty funny!" God's sense of humor is a bit warped at times. But I absolutely believe God does have a sense of humor, and He gets to use it in whatever way He wants.

On another occasion, I gave a message where I talked about faith and said the following: "We don't have to know the exact course of our journey to have faith. Actually, if we did know, it wouldn't require much faith at all. You've heard the phrase blind faith? I think it's descriptive in helping us understand walking by faith rather than by sight. But really I think ALL faith is blind faith. I don't think there's regular faith—and then blind faith for the super-spiritual. All faith is blind. It's believing for things that haven't happened yet. You may have heard of this example of faith. It says that all of you demonstrated faith this morning without even thinking about it when you sat down and trusted that the chair you're sitting on would hold you. Well, I'm sorry for any of you who like that illustration. But that's not faith! I've been sitting in chairs and seeing other people sit in chairs for over forty years. I don't need faith to believe that I can sit in a chair. Now take away the chair? And God says, "Have a seat!" And you sit down? Now that's faith!"

The very next day I returned to work and went over to my friend's office to talk to her. And I sat down in a chair that I had been sitting in for over 10 years. But on this day—one day after my very clever description of faith—do you know that chair came apart at the side and I almost landed on the floor? "Very funny God—very funny!" My guess is that He gathered a bunch of angels around to watch. "Here she comes—get ready—this is going to be hysterical!"

God greatly enjoys laughter and so should we. I am so very thankful for family, friends, a husband and a Savior who nurture my soul with humor again and again. And for a "cat," so to speak, who has provided me with some of my most amusing memories to date.

Your Story:

What about you? How often do you laugh? And I mean real, actual, from the gut, my stomach hurts belly-laughter. Do you laugh like that on a regular basis? I certainly recognize that there is much in life that is not at all humorous. Working, raising children, taking care of a home, fighting financial worries, health issues, and on and on. The busyness and the various stressors in life can weigh you down and often you may find yourself more ready to cry than laugh.

But the verse in Proverbs is true. A broken spirit will sap your strength and dry up your bones. If you're neglecting to feed your funny bone, eventually it's going to take a toll on your physical health. In contrast, laughter may indeed be the best medicine. Research shows that laughter can improve circulation, lower blood pressure, stabilize the heart rate, and increase blood oxygen levels. It's also been found that laughter suppresses the stress-related hormones in the brain and activates the immune system. T-cell, killer cell and white blood cell production are all increased along with the increased production of other immune system cells including gamma-interferon, which is believed to fight cancer. The release of endorphins, which are natural painkillers, increases with laughter. And when we laugh, ten different muscle groups are exercised. They contract and relax in a way that performs a type of massage on our internal organs.

William Fry, Jr. has done research on the physiology of laughter for over fifty years and he says, "Laughter is like internal jogging." [2] So see—you can actually exercise without leaving the couch if you laugh hard enough! How great is that? Research has found that laughing one hundred times is equal to ten minutes on the rowing machine or fifteen minutes on an exercise bike. Laughter gives your diaphragm, abdominal, respiratory, facial, leg and back muscles a workout. That's why you often feel exhausted after a long bout of laughter—you've just had a total body aerobic workout. Now that sounds like my type of exercise!

And what do we usually say after a good laugh? "Oh, that felt great! It feels so good to laugh." Then sadly, "I haven't laughed like that in years." Or, "I can't remember the last time I laughed that hard—my side hurts." It shouldn't be years in between times when we have a good laugh.

---

[2] http://www.associatedcontent.com/article/1392659/maintain_your_health_with_laughter.html?cat=5

Here are some great quotes that I found on laughter:[3]

Laughter is an instant vacation. *~Milton Berle*

A man isn't poor if he can still laugh. *~Raymond Hitchcock*

What soap is to the body, laughter is to the soul. *~Yiddish Proverb*

A smile starts on the lips, A grin spreads to the eyes, A chuckle comes from the belly; But a good laugh bursts forth from the soul, overflows, and bubbles all around. *~Carolyn Birmingham*

Against the assault of laughter nothing can stand. *~Mark Twain*

It is impossible for you to be angry and laugh at the same time. Anger and laughter are mutually exclusive and you have the power to choose either. *~Dr. Wayne Dyer*

If you are not allowed to laugh in heaven, I don't want to go there. *~Martin Luther*

I'm with Martin Luther. I am convinced that there will be much guffawing in Heaven. But we don't need to wait until we get there to enjoy the benefits of humor. If you're not belly laughing on a regular basis, I urge you to start. Laughter may not come as easily to you as it did to my Grandma. But I strongly encourage you to find your sense of humor and develop it. Explore what's funny to you and what makes you laugh—and then actively seek opportunities to put yourself in those situations on a regular basis. Maybe it's watching old comedies on TV, hanging out with a friend or pet with a great sense of humor, or re-telling old stories for the hundredth time. Whatever it is, make laughter a part of your everyday life. Your body will thank you for it—and those around you will benefit as well.

---

[3] http://behappy4life.com/laughterquotes.html

Chapter 8

He was manipulative...
Know there is a better way

Knick's Story:

Although Knick could certainly be a barrel of laughs, our boy was also quite a force to be reckoned with. He wanted things done his way, right now, all the time. Obviously food was Knick's main priority and his incessant meowing was the top choice in his arsenal of manipulative tactics. But it wasn't his only tool.

On any given evening, if the continuous yapping wouldn't get it done, he'd switch to more pitiful, quiet maneuvers. Out of the corner of my eye, I'd see a silent but pleading cat figure from across the room. Not making so much as a whisper and with the most piteous look imaginable spread across his broad face, he'd sit. First lifting one striped paw up in the air, curled slightly towards his body, and then the other paw, back and forth, up and down, in an endless, hopeful petition that maybe, just maybe, someone would come to his aid.

Although unbelievably cute and much preferable to the loud-mouthed pleas, Knick's silent begging also yielded him no results. Undaunted, he'd pull out the most threatening option from his bag of tricks. With a very loud and angry *"MAWR,"* he'd march off towards the kitchen. Sidling right up to the beautiful, braided rug under the dining room table, handmade by my mother, he'd raise a furry foot one-half inch from the wool. Claws exposed, and with a most defiant expression, he'd look back toward the living room. *"I'm going to pick!"*

"KNICK!!!," I'd scream, racing towards him. "You pick at that rug and 'Grandma' will come declaw you herself, one toenail at a time."

"MAWR!!!!"

Usually that was the end of it and I'd go back to my recliner and the beggar cat would move on to something else as well. But sometimes his rage would get the best of him. We didn't always see the full show, as he'd usually wait until he was alone again, but we could hear him. Spinning in circles, with a mix of meows and hisses filling the air, Knick would vent his frustrations. Doug and I always wondered if that's how the term "hissy-fit" originated.

Another classic "Knick trick" involved pretending that he hadn't been fed yet. This strategy came in handy when our schedules were changed for some reason and Doug and I were in and out of the house but not home at the same time. Our slick friend would then try to pull the old "poor starving kitty routine." He never succeeded with this, but one of his attempts made the list of my all-time favorite Knick stories.

I arrived home from work one day and knew that Doug had already been home, but had then left again to run a quick errand. Knick, of course, figured I wasn't up to speed on any of this. Knowing that I typically feed him as soon as I come in the door, he went to his dish to await the blessed event. When it didn't come, he launched into his standard verbal lament. *"Meow, meow, meow, meow..."*

"Knickie, I'm pretty sure that you've already been fed."

"MEOW!"

Back and forth we went, both stating our cases with growing intensity as the minutes passed. Then we heard it together—a 1987 Saab coming up the driveway. "Well, I guess we'll find out the truth pretty soon, now won't we?" I went outside to greet Doug and obtain the verdict. Knick just looked stricken. When I came back in, my debating partner was drinking from his dish like he'd just spent forty days in the desert. He wouldn't even look up at me. "So, do you have anything to say for yourself?"

"Lap, lap, lap, lap, lap, lap, lap...I'm drinking...lap, lap, lap, lap..." After slurping enough to fill two camel's humps, he went silently on his way, never uttering another sound.

Not wanting to be one-dimensional, Knick was also manipulative about things other than food. Like if we weren't all in our expected places in the evening, he couldn't rest. I was to be on the recliner and Doug on the sofa. On occasions when I had the audacity to be at the computer in the back room, Knick's whole cat world was thrown out of kilter. Fortunately, he could see me from his place in the living room through that window that opened up into our little office. Unfortunately, I could hear him. *"Meow, meow, meow, meow..."* When I'd finally finish up and get to my appointed place, all would be well. And very often, I'd quickly have a large friend sharing my seat with me.

Knick absolutely LOVED to be held! As much as he'd yap for food, he'd also meow to be held. Since Doug's lap was bigger than mine was, he had an easier time of it. But most times, since I was in the recliner, and since I was me, mine was the chosen lap. Stretched from my stomach down to my ankles, my momma's boy lay, sound asleep in no time and purring to beat the band. I loved it as much as he did.

There's nothing so relaxing as stroking soft kitty fur and watching them sleep. But after an hour...or maybe two hours...my legs would become restless and I just had to move around. Undeterred, Knick would just reposition himself and continue snoozing. Eventually, I wouldn't be able to take it anymore and would just have to get up. And Knick would let out the most pitiful moan imaginable. Then in the same way that he wouldn't slide out of his cat carrier, he would somehow stay stuck to my legs. Either Doug or I could get our legs to nearly a standing position, and still have 18 pounds of cat velcroed to our laps. How Knick could defy gravity like that, I'll never quite understand.

But in spite of our Knickie's manipulative ways, we loved him unconditionally. How could we not? He was ours: for good or for bad—for loud or for quiet. We were a family. And our 3-fold cord was not easily broken.

My Story:

What an example, huh? Whether human or animal, we creatures all have our manipulative tendencies. Knick just so happened to paint a pretty classic picture of them. We want something from someone, whether it be a spouse, parent, friend or even God. So we ask for it. When that doesn't get the person's attention, we ask louder and longer. "Please, please, please, please..." *"Meow, meow, meow, meow..."* If our need still hasn't been met, we might move to the next stage—the silent, begging, pitiful tactic. If it still seems like we're being ignored, we move on to anger. "Fine—

have it your way!" And we stomp off in a snit to throw our own little hissy-fit.

I'm sorry to say that I definitely have a controlling-type personality. I love to have things go the way that I think they should. Generally I use more of a quieter, passive-aggressive technique than a loud, angry style. But the concept is the same. I'm hoping to control the situation and get my own way. Usually it's over small, inconsequential circumstances that don't even matter in the larger scheme of life. But there's something in me that longs for that sense of control. So it's a constant struggle for me to simply step back and let go of things. Doug has been very patient and forgiving with me in this area and he's also been a great teacher and encourager in helping me to break some of these tendencies.

With God, I don't struggle quite so much, maybe because I know it will be a losing battle. I recognize that I can't control Him. But that definitely doesn't lessen my frustration when He doesn't intervene when or how I think He should. I am pleased to say that I've never gotten so angry with God that I've completely walked away from Him. I've also never had the "vending machine" concept of Him. Where you make bargains or think if you do just the right thing at just the right time, that out will pop the exact result that you want? Our Lord is not so easily manipulated. But I certainly have had my moments of disappointment and discouragement during some long years of trials and much waiting.

In 2002, Doug was laid off from his job and decided to try to start his own business. We knew there were lots of risks in doing that, but we also felt God's leading. So with much prayer and a sense of anticipation, we set off on our journey. Along the way, there were numerous times when the situation looked hopeless. And like Knick, I sometimes felt like my petitions were being ignored. "God, don't You see me? Don't You hear me? We need Your help here." Well just like I saw and heard Knick (how could I miss him?), God saw and heard me. And each time we thought there was absolutely no answer to a problem, a solution would come about. Yet in the end, things did not work out as we had hoped. So two years later, with a pile of debt and a mountain of disappointment, the business dream came to an end.

In order to help manage things financially, we decided to sell our house and move to a rental property. Our home sold after one day on the market, so a month later we were in the new place. Shortly after that, my maternal Grandma died. Then I figured things would get better. They didn't. The next five years brought even greater trials—Doug's twin brother passed away, there was physical illness, emotional struggles, unemployment, and more discouragement than I cared to think about.

During much of that time all I wanted to do was cry and worry and feel sorry for myself. And I did some of that—and felt a whole lot worse. But when I forced myself to put the praise music on and raise my hands in worship in the living room, God was right there. My circumstances didn't change one bit. But my heart did. And I found a sweetness that can only come from rejoicing in the midst of trials.

But it's so hard to keep rejoicing when our situations don't change. More than once I became angry with God and told Him so. "You know what? It doesn't seem to matter what I do. I can praise You; I can ignore You. We're still having the same problems. You just do what You want anyway, so heck with it."

Rather than praising—begging, pleading and manipulating seemed to be more of a natural response. Along with asking why. "Why did all of this happen? What's the point? Why do things seem to keep getting worse instead of better? Why did the business fail, especially after we had prayed and trusted and followed Your leading to the best of our abilities?" Again and again, I just kept saying, "God, I don't understand."

In hindsight, I now have a better understanding of some things. At that time, I never got an explanation. But I did read Psalm 33:4 over and over and over again. "For the word of the Lord holds true, and everything He does is worthy of our trust." (NLT)

Everything, <u>everything</u> He does is worthy of our trust. It's not up to God to explain it all to us. It's up to us to trust Him. It's up to us to let God be God and to believe that He really does know best. At one point in my whining, I felt God asking me, "Would you have loved Me more if the business had been successful?" And I had to respond, "Yes, I think so," because I was so hurt and disappointed. I wasn't sure I really wanted to keep loving a God who would let me down like that, after all the hope and faith I had placed in Him. But He said, "Will you love Me for who I am—not because of what I give you? Will you love Me no matter what?" And my answer was, "Yes, I'll love You no matter what. I'll love You even when I don't understand. I'll love You when it's hard. I'll trust that You know what you're doing and I'll give up trying to figure out the plan. Because I can't figure it out."

We can throw as many hissy-fits as we want. We can cajole and manipulate and carry on till the cows come home. But God is going to work in His time and in His way. And He is going to love us throughout the entire process. Doug and I absolutely adored Knick. We loved him to the core of our beings. It positively broke our hearts to see him angry, upset or suffering in some way. But our best response was just to love him through the hard times. We couldn't always give him everything he wanted, but we could always give him our hearts. And Knick gave us his in return.

And that's how we need to approach our relationship with God, our eternal Caretaker. He's not always going to give us everything we want. And as much as we would like to, we can't always control our circumstances. But we can give God our hearts. And in return—He gives us His.

Our Lord will not be manipulated. And I'm so grateful that He won't. As rough as our journey has been, we've seen much fruit harvested along the way that never would have happened if I had gotten my own way. I'm thankful that God is always patient and kind with me, no matter how large or small of a hissy-fit I might throw. His loving presence is always there. And anytime I want, I can curl up and rest on my Papa's warm lap—and He'll never get tired of holding me.

Your Story:

Now it's your turn. Are you the manipulative kind, always trying to get your own way? Do you yell and hiss and carry on when your plans don't work out? Or are you more of the silent, begging, pleading type? Maybe like me, you have more of a quiet, passive-aggressive manner to maneuver your way around situations or people. Whatever your style, I would venture to say that we all have a bit of this Knick characteristic in us. It's simply part of our sinful human nature. But being aware of it can greatly help us to interact with others with more of a loving nature rather than in a manipulative way.

Understanding these tendencies will help in your interactions with God as well. What kind of manipulative tactics have you tried with Him? Do you get angry and frustrated when He doesn't answer in the manner or timing that you think He should? Do you know that He loves you anyway? Do you understand that God is not upset when you vent your honest frustrations to Him? He knows how you're feeling and what you're thinking regardless. It's all part of the sincere relationship that He desires to have with each one of us.

When you can let go of the desire for control and take hold of the choice to rejoice and trust in Him no matter your circumstances, it will go a long way in your journey of faith. If you can get it settled in your heart that God truly is good and that He really does know what's best for you—at all times and in every situation—then you can read Romans 8:28 and really believe it. "And we know that God causes everything to work together for the good of those who love God and are called according to His purpose for them." (NLT) Or say with Job, "Though he slay me, yet will I trust in Him." (Job 13:15, KJV)

When life wears you down and you get tired of waiting; when God seems to be moving much too slowly for your needs, it's easy to try and take matters into your own hands and let the frustration bubble over. "Okay God—you know what? You had your chance. I trusted You, but nothing's worked out. Obviously either I missed something along the way or You really don't come through the way You're supposed to—at least not in my life anyway." With that, we then set out on our own and muddle along as good as we can. And I believe we miss out on God's best. We leave Him standing there with His arms outstretched, saying, "If you had just kept going—you have NO idea what was in store just around the next bend!"

If you're going to make it through the long journey of perseverance that life often seems to bring, you have got to stay on the road however tempting it might be to get off and begin to chart your own path and take control of your circumstances. If you have done all you know to do—if God has shown you that He is taking you down this road, then keep going. Don't make God too small by deciding you need to figure it out for Him. Let Him be big. Because we serve a big God! Deuteronomy says this, "Understand therefore, that the Lord your God is indeed God. He is the faithful God who keeps His covenant for a thousand generations and constantly loves those who love Him and obey His commands." (Deuteronomy 7:9, NLT)

You need to grasp this. God is the same—yesterday, today, and tomorrow. The same God who created the earth, who rescued Noah from the flood, who kept His promise to Abraham, who did miracle upon miracle, who came Himself as a baby, died, and rose again so that we could have eternal life with Him—that is the God who loves you! That is the God you're trusting in. Nothing is too hard for Him and no one is beyond His reach. He loves you—He loves me—and He sees us right where we are—in the middle of our messes. And He says, "I'll take care of you. I will never leave you; I will never forsake you."

His promises remain true, no matter how we respond to them. So whether you praise Him or attempt to manipulate Him, God loves you unconditionally. How could He not? He created you. And He's yours: in your good and your bad—your loud and your quiet. And He longs for you to join His family—where a 3-fold cord is not easily broken.

Chapter 9

He was spiritual...
Develop your relationship with God

Knick's Story:

Even when he was a kitten, I always talked to Knick as though he were a person. In fact, I pretty much will talk to any animal in that manner. Most of the time, the squirrels or rabbits that I might encounter along the way just give me a passing glance at best. Although there was that duck... One day I was taking a walk and happened upon a female mallard standing in someone's driveway—and laughing her head off! The sound and cadence of her quacks combined with the way she was moving her head and the shape of her beak absolutely made it appear as though she was laughing hysterically. So I decided to join her. No doubt I stood there for a good three to four minutes laughing with that duck. I was doubled over it was so hilarious. I have no idea what she thought was so funny but it certainly lightened my mood.

Anyway, back to Knick. The difference with him was not only that he talked back to me. He would also listen—intently—as though he was looking straight into my soul. I distinctly remember one day when he was still quite little. We were in the bedroom and I was babbling on about who knows what and I happened to glance down. There was my kitty—baby blue eyes fixed on mine and attentive to my every word—like he cared! I recall thinking, "Oh my gosh, he's looking at me as if to say," *"You're my mama. I'm listening."* And he never stopped listening. That's not to say the fuzz-butt was always completely obedient—what child is? But I felt like for the most part, he understood pretty much whatever we told him. Doug scoffed at this idea until he was soundly proven otherwise.

In the early going, he and Knickie were prone to roughhousing. Doug would pet him in a playful manner and Knick would subsequently bite at his hand. Never having owned a cat before, my husband was quite distressed that this new addition to the family would have the audacity to jump up on the table or counters whenever he pleased. With a bit of training, Doug figured this could be resolved. So he began to lightly swat him whenever Knick displayed bad kitty behavior. I quickly told Doug to stop but he persisted for a time, still thinking his techniques would yield success. Finally, with a bit firmer resolve, I explained to my spouse that you should never hit a cat. I told him that they absolutely do not learn in that way and that it was clear that Knickerbocker was becoming frightened. Doug then understood and completely stopped any and all forms of punishment.

Knick very quickly became comfortable again and any fear of interacting with us was completely gone. However, not surprisingly, he continued to bite at Doug's hands whenever he tried to pet him, no matter how gentle a manner and voice he might use. So on that most memorable of days, our stout tabby was standing in the living room and Doug came over to sweetly pet him. Knick of course, began his usual hand gnawing. Exasperated, Doug said to me, "I'm tired of him always biting me like this. I'd like to just be able to pet him without him always hurting me."

"Then you need to apologize to him," I offered.

"What? Are you out of your mind? I am NOT going to apologize to a cat!"

"Well," I said, "then I guess you're never going to have any sort of relationship with him. It's your choice."

With a heavy sigh and an incredulous look, my husband got down on his knees. While continuing to stroke Knickie's fur he said, "Knick—I apologize for being mean to you. I promise that I'll never hit you again. I'm sorry." Not during the entire act of repentance nor ever again did Knick bite at Doug's hands. From that moment forward, Doug could pet or hold him however he wished and there was not one ounce of aggression. In fact, in the years to come, my boys became the best of friends. To say Doug was astonished by the whole apology scenario is putting it mildly. I wasn't surprised in the least.

For me, Knickie was like my soulmate from day one. He used to sleep on my pillow above my head until he grew so large that he was as big as the pillow and my choice was to either scrunch down below him or attempt to sleep with at least fifteen pounds of purring cat blubber covering my head. Thankfully, Knick also realized this was no longer working and made the switch to the other end. My friend then developed the most wonderful habit of pressing his wide back right up against my little feet. When my soles were set firmly on his solid body, all was right with the world.

Also, anytime my furry buddy was lying anywhere, I could lay down with him and gently rest my head on him and he never flinched. A soft, warm, fuzzy purring pillow is absolutely the best! Our nighttime routine became that Knickie would go lie down on the loveseat in the spare room upstairs. After finishing up in the bathroom, I would go in and curl up beside him, wrap my arms around his girth and lay my head on his soft body. Then I'd whisper in his ear, "You're my first best cat," while listening to his purring motor and feeling his soft fur against my face. After a few minutes, I'd go next door to bed and he'd shortly join me, taking his place at my feet.

Not only was Knick a great sleeping buddy, he was also a wonderful source of comfort during our difficult times. I could pour out my problems to my feline friend and he'd never interrupt. Much as he loved to chat, he also knew when to be silent. When I was having a rough time, not even one meow would pass through those lips while I bared my soul. There were several occasions when I just wrapped my arms around his strong, triangular frame and cried my eyes out. And my sweet boy would sit there stoically, not moving a muscle, for as long as I needed him to remain in place.

Knick had a remarkable ability to seemingly appear out of nowhere—and usually it would happen when Doug and I would also happen to suddenly be sharing the same space. For instance one of us might be in the kitchen and next thing you know, the other of us would somehow have an urgent need to complete a task in that exact same area of the kitchen at the exact same time. Usually before Doug could let out a sigh of frustration, we'd look down and there would be the third member of the trinity. Always with a questioning look like, *"Why are we all here? What are we doing?"* Then we'd go through what became our standard verbal routine. Doug would say, "Here we are—all within 3 inches of each other." Then I would repeat, "1-2-3… I count 3." Strangely enough, Knick didn't have a line. You would have thought he'd have come up with something but he never did. He would just continue to look up with his head on a swivel, still puzzled as to why we were all unexpectedly in the same place.

Our boy also had a wonderful habit of joining in on Sunday evenings when we'd have friends over. We used to meet weekly with two other couples from church to lift up the prayer requests of those in our fellowship. We would alternate among our homes so every few weeks it would be our turn. As expected, Knick would be right there to stare at our friends and make sure they remained on their best behavior. Usually during the time when we'd make small talk and catch up with each other, he would be in the living room but maybe at more of a distance or sometimes he'd briefly lounge on the soft blue felt inside Ron's guitar case. However, when the chatting and singing had ended and it was time to pray, there was never a Sunday when Knick didn't suddenly appear in the circle. And there he'd quietly remain until the prayer time was concluded.

One Saturday when Doug and I decided to spend some time in prayer, Knickie made another quite memorable appearance. We were in the midst of our trials and felt that we needed to take a few minutes to lift some things up to our Father. So we went upstairs to the spare room and sat down on the carpet. I have no idea where Knick had been as I hadn't seen him anywhere—until he suddenly and immediately appeared in our little circle of three. We held hands and/or paws as the case may be and then we began. I prayed, Doug prayed and then Knick began purring softly. It was truly remarkable.

My Story:

My faith has always been a vital part of my life. And how awesome it's been to not only have a husband to share my spiritual journey with but to have also had a pet who far exceeded my expectations in so many ways. That day at the shelter, I thought I was just picking out a stray kitten. Turns out I was choosing a friend and soulmate who would forever change my life. Knick's love, forgiveness and friendship will never be forgotten. I am so very thankful to God for bringing us a furry partner who helped to complete our little family of three.

Whenever we would all end up at the same place in the house together, I couldn't help but think of Matthew 18:20. "For where two or three are gathered together in my name, there am I in the midst of them." (KJV) Whenever we had two, we had three; but actually we had even more than that. Because God was there with us as well through the Holy Spirit. God loves keeping company with us. Whether it was opening Christmas gifts, sitting in a prayer circle or simply making a sandwich, we enjoyed the fellowship of each other and of our Lord.

God loves fellowship—so much so that He designed the Trinity—Father, Son and Holy Spirit, three in one. He designed us for fellowship with Him as well as with each other. We were not meant to live in isolation. We were intended to live in communion with others—to offer love, forgiveness and friendship.

There is no doubt in my mind that we would never have survived the difficulties that we went through without the love and support of our many friends. They faithfully stood by our sides, both literally and figuratively, year after year after year. They loved without judgment, gave without expectation and cared without pity. Our friends were simply there for us—rock solid, unmovable support, that we could lean on and cry with for as long as necessary, just as Knick was there for me in my most desperate times.

And just as our friends were there for us, God was there as well. When I placed my feet upon Knick's strong body every night, it was a symbol to me of my unwavering faith in Christ, the Solid Rock. Isaiah 28:16 says, "Therefore the Lord God said: 'Look, I have laid a stone in Zion, a tested stone, a precious cornerstone, a sure foundation; the one who believes will be unshakable.' " (HCSB) As difficult as our circumstances were, and although I had plenty of moments of doubt and uncertainty in how things might turn out, deep down inside, I had an unshakeable, unmovable faith.

A number of years ago, as part of the Sunday morning message, our pastor had each person come forward and choose a small stone, symbolic of God being our rock, a stronghold and place of refuge. I kept the stone on my dresser as a reminder. Some time later, at a church meeting, the group leader had little plastic feet, hands and lips, symbols of various ways of serving. We were asked to choose whichever one we wished. I chose a foot. After bringing it home, I was in the bedroom and noticed the stone on my dresser. My immediate thought was, "I'm going to glue that foot to my rock— because my soles are planted firmly—and I will not be shaken!" I love looking at that stone. It's a daily reminder to me of the firm foundation that I'm standing on—one that will never be moved.

Christ is indeed our Solid Rock. He is also the source of love and compassion and forgiveness if we make the choice to have a relationship with Him. Doug could have continued on with his contentious relationship with Knick. But he decided that he wanted more. Doug was skeptical at best when he got down on his knees. He had absolutely no expectation that anything positive would come of it, though he was entirely sincere in his repentance. Doug truly was sorry for how he had treated Knick. He had just never told him so directly. When he did—the results were astonishing.

After that day, Doug and Knick had a new and lasting friendship. During the many long days toiling over the business in the back room, Knick was right there by Doug's side. Yes, often sleeping, but there nonetheless. Knickie became a source of love, comfort and companionship to my husband that he never would have had if he had not asked for Knick's forgiveness. When Knick became ill, Doug cried and pleaded with God to not take away his friend.

I've often heard the phrase that we can be "Jesus with skin on" to other people. I believe without a doubt that God does indeed intend for us to love and care for each other so that Christ's love comes shining through. But I also think that every now and then—His love comes with fur on.

Your Story:

Who are you keeping company with? Who's in your circle of friends? Do you have companions that you can count on to love you and support you no matter what? Or when things go wrong are they the first ones to criticize, question or give you advice that you don't really want or need? What kind of friend are you? How do you react when someone you care about is going through a troubled time? Do you provide quiet, heartfelt compassion for as long as it takes? Or are you the first one to jump in with an idea or opinion?

One concept that is very important to keep in mind when difficult circumstances arise is that the person who is going through the difficulty is separate from the trial itself. It's vital, especially during hard times, that we recognize who we are. And who we are not. It's so easy to get caught up in seeing ourselves as the problem. Whether it's illness, divorce, financial issues, you name it. When we start to apply labels and only see ourselves or others in terms of the situation, we're in trouble.

I can't stress enough how important it is to just accept people for who they are, regardless of their circumstances. Love them, cry with them, embrace them, encourage them. If your friend needs a shoulder to cry on, let them wrap their arms around you and bawl for as long as it takes—while you do nothing but sit there steadily and quietly until they've finished.

God is with us in many ways when we're hurting. He is with us Himself through His Holy Spirit. But He might also provide loving friends, family, a church body, or maybe even a pet. Who are you leaning on? Are your feet planted on a firm foundation? Or are you standing on unsteady ground? Hebrews 12:12-13 tells us, "So take a new grip with your tired hands and stand firm on your shaky legs. Mark out a straight path for your feet. Then those who follow you, though they are weak and lame, will not stumble and fall but will become strong." (NLT)

When you glue your soles to the Rock, you will have firm footing in which to continue your life's journey. Then no matter what happens, you will know that you are standing on solid ground. Not only will you find strength for your own walk—you'll also encourage those around you. You can provide an example of faith, courage and hope for your friends, family, neighbors and co-workers. No matter what your circumstances, there is always reason to hope.

Romans 5 says, "Therefore, since we have been made right in God's sight by faith, we have peace with God because of what Jesus Christ our Lord has done for us. Because of our faith, Christ has brought us into this place of highest privilege where we now stand, and we confidently and joyfully look forward to sharing God's glory. We can rejoice, too, when we run into problems and trials, for we know that they are good for us—they help us learn to endure. And endurance develops strength of character in us, and character strengthens our confident expectation of salvation. And this expectation will not disappoint us. For we know how dearly God loves us, because He has given us the Holy Spirit to fill our hearts with His love. When we were utterly helpless, Christ came at just the right time and died for us sinners. Now, no one is likely to die for a good person, though someone might be willing to die for a person who is especially good. But God showed His great love for us by sending Christ to die for us while we were still sinners. And since we have been made right in God's sight by the blood of Christ, He will certainly save us from God's judgment. For since we were restored to friendship with God by the death of His Son while we were still His enemies, we will certainly be delivered from eternal punishment by His life. So now we can rejoice in our wonderful new relationship with God—all because of what our Lord Jesus Christ has done for us in making us friends of God." (Romans 5:1-11, NLT)

God longs for you to be part of His family. But you'll never know what that relationship can be like if you don't take that first step of repentance. If you've never done so, put aside your skepticism, your doubts and your unbelief. Get down on your knees in front of your Creator and offer a sincere apology for how you've treated Him. Tell Him that from this day forward, you'd like to have a brand new relationship with Him. One where you'll treat Him with the love and kindness and respect that He deserves. Then stand back in wonder and awe at the amazing results you'll see and feel as you enter into fellowship with the greatest Friend and soulmate you'll ever know— One who will forever change your life.

Epilogue

...but he was never a cat.

Fulfill your purpose

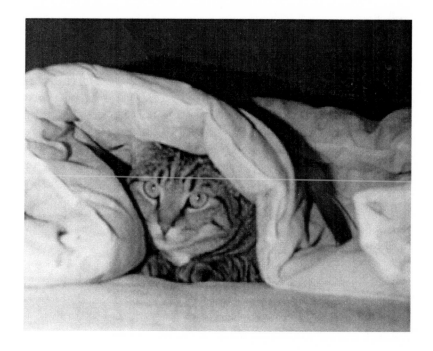

Knick's Story:

At the same time as the business was coming to a close, Knick's kidney disease that he had been battling for over five years was finally getting the best of him. More pitiful than anything else was that our sweet friend completely lost his appetite. For the first time in his life, our furry companion had full permission to eat anything and everything that he could possibly want. And he hardly enjoyed a bite of it.

We tried everything. The vet gave us oodles of free samples of every cat food imaginable. We gave him little plates with chicken and pork chops and cheese—all his favorites. He could have as many kitty treats as his little heart desired. But the best our buddy could do was to take a few nibbles and walk away. It absolutely broke our hearts.

Our days with Knickerbocker were coming to an end and there was no denying it. So on March 23, 2004, one day prior to putting our house on the market, we scheduled Knick's final visit to Dr. Bill's. For several weeks leading up to that day, Knickie would spend the majority of his time curled up asleep on a blanket in the back corner of the bedroom, leaving his spot only to use the litter box. But on his last night with us, our tabby friend made the complete rounds of all his old routines. He spent some time on his table in the back room snoozing and looking out the window. Then to my utter surprise, he stood by the back door and meowed. Outside we went for one last visit on the deck to take in some fresh air and a brief look around. Within a few minutes, the striped one led the way back inside. That evening as I relaxed in the recliner, suddenly a familiar weight landed on my lap. And I was determined to not move a muscle until my best friend decided he was ready to get down. We sat there together for most of the evening while I stroked his still soft, yet clearly ailing, fur.

The next afternoon I went upstairs to get Knickie for the last leg of his journey. He was lying on the floor in the spare room and although much lighter than his previous weight, my boy made himself so heavy that I could barely lift him off the carpet. Finally I managed to scoop him up and told him over and over again that we would be brave together. And we were.

For the first time ever, Knick slid into his carrier with not so much as a whimper. A kind friend volunteered to drive us to the vet's and Knick remained calm for the entire trip. After removing the top part of his carrier, the tech took him to the back room for preparation. Again, he never made a sound.

When they brought him back, Knickie was nestled contentedly in the bottom part of his carrier, his body forming a perfect loaf, as he rested on a soft, pale yellow comforter adorned with stars and moons. He was completely at peace. I stroked his fur and told him how much he had meant to me. Then one last time, I wrapped my arms around my sweet boy and whispered in his ear, "You're my first best cat." But we both knew it wasn't true. He was never a cat. He was Knick. And for that, I am eternally grateful.

Our Story:

We all have a story. And we all have significance— human and animal alike. None of us are here by accident. God designed each life for a unique calling and an individualized purpose. Psalm 139 says that God knew us before we were even born. "For you created my inmost being; you knit me together in my mother's womb. I praise you because I am fearfully and wonderfully made; your works are wonderful, I know that full well. My frame was not hidden from you when I was made in the secret place. When I was woven together in the depths of the earth, your eyes saw my unformed body. All the days ordained for me were written in your book before one of them came to be." (Psalm 139:13-16, NIV)

Even before the creation of the world, God saw each one of us. And He has loved us—from the beginning of time. His deepest longing is for us to love Him in return and to live our lives in such a way that they would bring Him glory. He also desires that we fulfill the purposes for which He has created us.

We each have only one life—many chances throughout our lives—but only one life to fulfill the hopes, dreams, and purposes to which we have been called. There is no doubt in my mind that Knickerbocker fulfilled the role that the Lord had for him. I may falter and struggle, but my aim is to continue pressing on in the ways God is calling me. How about you? Are you living your life with purpose? Do you love others and accept them just the way they are? Do you hunger to be all you were created to be?

Thank you for listening to our stories—and for writing your own. As you go, I pray you take a bit of Knick and me with you on your journey—and that together, we can all bring glory to the greatest Storyteller ever.

9 781609 104696